W9-BIW-991

SRA Art Connections

Level 2

Authors

Rosalind Ragans, Ph.D., Senior Author

Willis Bing Davis
Tina Farrell
Jane Rhoades Hudak, Ph.D.
Gloria McCoy
Bunyan Morris
Nan Yoshida

Contributing Writer

Faye Scannell

Music Center Education Division
The Music Center of Los Angeles County

Columbus, Ohio

A Division of The McGraw·Hill Companies

Credits

Cover, André Derain, *The Turning Road, L'Estaque*, Museum of Fine Arts, Houston, Texas. The John A. and Audrey Jones Beck Collection; **Back Cover**, top Sarah Leggett, Age 7, *A Relaxing Afternoon*; middle Jessie Little, Age 6, *The Pink Tree*; bottom Brian Magelssen, Age 7, *Screen Saver*; **13**, The Metropolitan Museum of Art, NY. Gift of Countess Bismarck, 1961; **26**, Photo courtesy of AMAN International Folk Ensemble; **29**, Photo courtesy of the Los Angeles County Museum of Art, ©1997; **31**, ©Sylvain Grandadam, Photo Researchers Inc.; **44**, Photo by Ken Howard, ©1993; **47**, Photo by Brian Seed/Black Star; **49**, Photo courtesy of UPI/Corbis-Bettmann; **62**, Photo by Deborah Allison; **65**, Photo ©1987 by Alan McGee. Courtesy of the High Museum of Art, Atlanta, GA; **67**, Photo by Michiko Matsumoto. Courtesy of the Pace Wildenstein Gallery, NY; **80**, Illustration by Nancy Walker, courtesy of The Robert Minden Ensemble; **83**, Photo courtesy of Pei, Cobb, Freed and Partners; **85**, Andrew Mellon Collection, ©1996 Board of Trustees, National Gallery of Art, Washington, DC; **98**, Photo by Mark Fellman. Courtesy of the Korean Classical Music and Dance Company; **101**, ©Superstock; **103**, Gift of Betty and Jack Bogart. Photo ©1996. The Avery Brundage Collection. Asian Art Museum of San Francisco, CA; **116**, Drawing courtesy of Remy Charlip, ©1991, Remy Charlip; **119**, Photo courtesy of Albert Romero; **140**, *Pagoda of the Temple of the Six Banyon Trees,* Guangzhou, China. K. Scholz/H. Armstrong Roberts; *Notre Dame de Paris (South Flank)* , ©1995 James F. Palka/Nawrocki Stock Photo, Inc. All Rights Reserved; *Tutankhamen Mask (Side View)*, ©Brian Brake, Photo Researchers; *Acropolis,* Athens, Greece. ©Vladimir Pcholkin/FPG International Corp.; **141**, *Stonehenge*, ©1984 Lawrence Migdale/Photo Researchers, Inc.; *Yellow Horse*, ©Douglas Mazonowicz/Gallery of Prehistoric Art; *Adena Effigy figure (Adena Pipe)*, Courtesy of the Ohio Historical Society; *Shiva as Lord of the Dance*, The Asia Society, New York, Mr. and Mrs. John D. Rockefeller 3rd Collection/Photo by Lynton Gardiner; *Ravenna Apse Mosaic (Detail)*, Scala, Art Resource, NY; *Hamiwa Figure: Horse,* Japan, Kofun, 5-6th century AD. Terra-cotta, 58.4 x 66 cm. ©The Cleveland Museum of Art, 1996, Norweb Collection, 1957.27; **142**, Leonardo da Vinci, *Mona Lisa*, Louvre, Paris, France. Erich Lessing, Art Resource, NY; Claude Monet, *Impression, Sunrise*, Musee Marmottan, Paris, France. Giraudon/Art Resource, NY; Michelangelo Buonarroti, *Head of David*, Scala, Art Resource, NY; Jan Vermeer, *Girl with the Red Hat*, National Gallery of Art, Washington, DC. Andrew W. Mellon Collection, ©1996 Board of Trustees, National Gallery of Art, Washington DC; Albrecht Dürer, *Self Portrait*, Museo del Prado, Madrid, Spain. Scala/Art Resource, NY; **143**, *Taj Mahal*, ©The Telegraph Colour Library/FPG International Corp.; Vincent van Gogh, *Bedroom at Arles*, ©1996 Art Institute Chicago, Chicago, IL. Helen Birch Bartlett Memorial Collection, 1926.417. All Rights Reserved; Pablo Picasso, *Gertrude Stein*, ©1996 The Metropolitan Museum of Art, New York, NY. Bequest of Gertrude Stein, 1946, (47.106); Marc Chagall, *Peasant Life*, Albright-Knox Art Gallery, Buffalo, NY, Room of Contemporary Art Fund, 1941/©1998 Artists Rights Society (ARS), NY/ADAGP, Paris; Georgia O'Keeffe, *Cow's Skull: Red, White, and Blue*, The Metropolitan Museum of Art, New York, NY. Alfred Stieglitz Collection, 1952. ©1998 The Georgia O'Keeffe Foundation/Artists; **148**, Aaron Haupt/Aaron Haupt Photography; **150**, Michael Newman/PhotoEdit; **152**, Photo by Mark Burnet.

SRA/McGraw-Hill

A Division of The **McGraw·Hill** *Companies*

Send all inquiries to:
SRA/McGraw-Hill
250 Old Wilson Bridge Road
Suite 310
Worthington, Ohio 43085

Printed in the United States of America.

ISBN 0-02-688316-3

3 4 5 6 7 8 9 VHP 02 01 00 99

Authors
Senior Author
Dr. Rosalind Ragans, Ph. D.
Associate Professor Emerita
Georgia Southern University

Willis Bing Davis
Art Department Chair
Central State University, Ohio

Tina Farrell
Director of Visual and Performing Arts,
Clear Creek Independent School District, Texas

Jane Rhoades Hudak, Ph.D.
Professor of Art
Georgia Southern University

Gloria McCoy
K-12 Art Supervisor, Spring Branch Independent School District, Texas

Bunyan Morris
Demonstration Art Teacher
Marvin Pittman Laboratory School,
Georgia Southern University

Nan Yoshida
Former Art Supervisor,
Los Angeles Unified School District, California

Contributors ARTSOURCE Music, Dance, Theater Lessons
The Music Center of Los Angeles County Education Division, Los Angeles, California
Executive Director, Music Center Education Division–Joan Boyett
Concept Originator and Project Director–Melinda Williams
Project Coordinator–Susan Cambigue-Tracey
Arts Discipline Writers:
Dance–Susan Cambigue-Tracey
Music–Rosemarie Cook-Glover
Theater–Barbara Leonard
Staff Assistance–Victoria Bernal
Logo Design–Maureen Erbe

More About Aesthetics
Richard W. Burrows, Executive Director, Institute for Arts Education, San Diego, California

Safe Use of Art Materials
Mary Ann Boykin, Visiting Lecturer, Art Education; Director, The Art School for Children and Young Adults, University of Houston-Clear Lake, Houston, Texas

Museum Education
Marilyn JS Goodman, Director of Education,
Solomon R. Guggenheim Museum,
New York,New York

The National Museum of Women in the Arts Collection
National Museum of Women in the Arts,
Washington, DC

Contributing Writer
Faye Scannell
Art Specialist and Lead Technology Teacher
Bellevue School District
Bellevue, Washington

Reviewers
Mary Ann Boykin
Visiting Lecturer, Art Education;
Director, The Art School for Children and Young Adults
University of Houston-Clear Lake Houston, TX

Judy Gong
Multi-age Classroom Teacher
Pacific Elementary School
Lincoln Unified School District
Stockton, CA

Lori Groendyke Knutti
Art Educator
Harrison Street Elementary School
Big Walnut Elementary School
Sunbury, OH

Randall K. Martinez
Second Grade Teacher
Dellview Elementary School
North East Independent School District
San Antonio, TX

Steven R. Sinclair
Art Teacher
Big Country Elementary School
Southwest Independent School District
San Antonio, TX

Marian Kane Strauss
ESL Teacher
Beverly Hills Unified School District
Beverly Hills, CA

Student Activity Testers
Nicole Euchler
Ciera Vance
Samantha Trotter
Gary Clarke

TABLE OF CONTENTS

Unit 3 Color and Value

Unit 4 Movement and Rhythm

Unit 5 Balance, Texture, and Emphasis

Unit 6 Harmony, Variety, and Unity

More About . . .

What Is Art?

Art is . . .

Painting

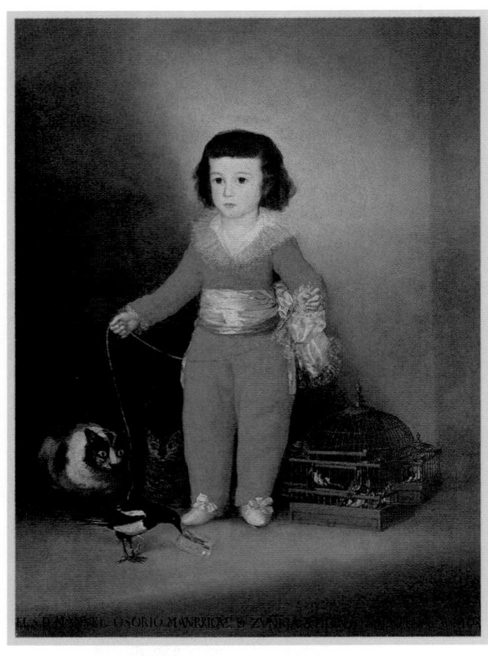

Francisco Goya. (Spanish). *Don Manuel Osorio Manrique de Zuñiga.* 1784. Oil on canvas. 50 × 40 inches. Metropolitan Museum of Art, New York, New York.

Architecture

Artist unknown. (Italy). *Pantheon.* A.D. 118–128. Concrete, brick, marble, and bronze. 141 feet high. Rome, Italy.

Sculpture

Roxanne Swentzell. (American). *The Emergence of the Clowns.* 1988. Coiled and scraped clay. A. 58.4 × 33 × 33 cm; B. 43.2 × 55.9 × 45.7 cm; C. 43.2 × 35.6 × 35.6 cm; D. 17.8 × 43.8 × 26 cm. Heard Museum, Phoenix, Arizona.

Drawing

Leonardo da Vinci. (Italian). *Self Portrait.* 1414. Red chalk. Royal Library, Turin, Italy, Scala, Art Resource, NY.

Printmaking

Thomas Hart Benton. (American). *I Got a Girl on Sourwood Mountain.* 1938. Lithograph. $12\frac{1}{2} \times 9\frac{1}{4}$ inches. © 1988 T.H. Benton and R.P. Benton Testamentary Trusts/Licensed by VAGA, New York, NY. Reproduced from the Collections of the Library of Congress, Washington, D.C.

Photography

Edward Steichen. (American). *The Flatiron—Evening.* 1904. Photograph. Metropolitan Museum of Art, New York, New York.

Pottery

Lucy Leuppe McKelvey. (American). *Whirling Rainbow Goddesses.* $6\frac{3}{4}$ inches tall, 12-inch diameter. Keams Canyon Arts and Crafts. New Mexico.

Puppets

Artist unknown. (Indonesia). *Indonesian Shadow Puppets.* c. 1950. Cut painted leather. $31\frac{1}{2}$ inches high. Private Collection.

Art is created by people.

Art talks with . . .

Line

Shape

Color

VALUE

SPACE

FORM

TEXTURE

Rhythm

Balance

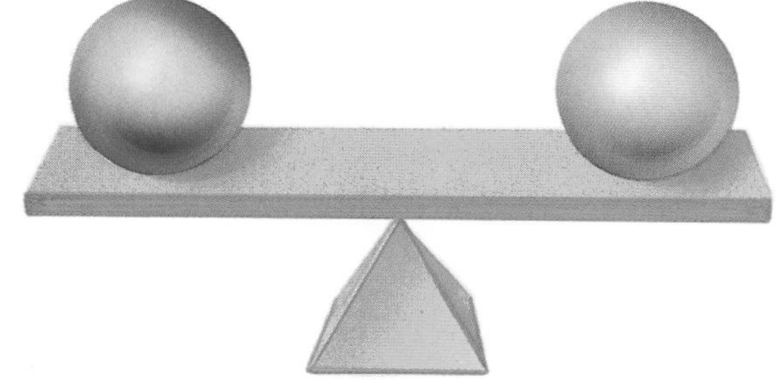

Emphasis

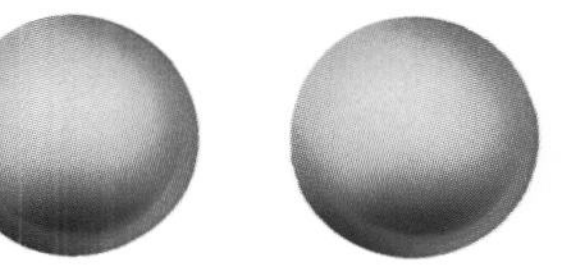

Variety

Harmony

Unity

Unit 1

An Introduction to Line and Shape

Francisco Goya. (Spanish). *Don Manuel Osorio Manrique de Zuñiga.* 1784. Oil on canvas. 50 × 40 inches. Metropolitan Museum of Art, New York, New York.

This artist uses different kinds of lines to make people, objects, and places.

- Look at these two paintings.
- Which objects in the paintings are made with curved lines?
- Which shapes are geometric?

Artist Profile

Francisco Goya. *(Spanish). José Costa y Bonells Pepito.*

Francisco Goya

- was a Spanish painter.
- began painting at age 14.
- liked to paint emotions, or feelings.
- painted both pictures on these pages.

In this unit you will:

- learn how artists use lines and shapes to show ideas and feelings.
- practice using lines and shapes to show ideas and feelings.

Lines Have Names

Heron Martínez. (Mexican). *Church.* c.1960. Painted earthenware. 24 inches high. From the Girard Foundation Collection, in the Museum of International Folk Art, a unit of the Museum of New Mexico, Santa Fe, New Mexico. Photographer: Michel Monteaux.

This is a **sculpture** of a Mexican church. Trace the outlines of the doors, windows, and shapes of this sculpture. What kinds of lines did the sculptor use to make them?

Seeing like an artist

Name things around your house with the same kinds of lines as the sculpture.

A line is named for the direction in which it moves.

vertical | horizontal | diagonal | zigzag

Create

Where do you see different line directions on a playground? Use different lines to design an exciting place to play.

1. Think about a place to climb, slide, hide, or swing.
2. Twist, curl, and fold strips of paper to make lines in space. Fold the ends of the strips for tabs and glue onto the paper.
3. Add people and objects, using scraps of paper.

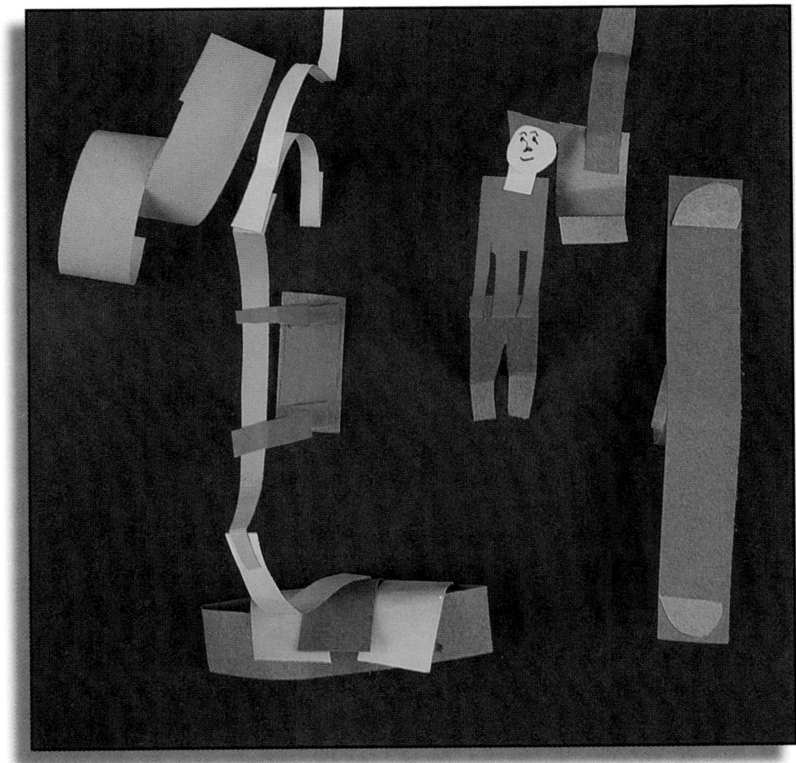

Anzlee Brock. Age 7. *The Playground.* Construction paper and marker.

Many Kinds of Lines

Joseph Stella. (American). *The Voice of the City of New York/ The White Way I.* 1920–22. Oil and tempera on canvas. $88\frac{1}{2} \times 54$ inches. Collection of The Newark Museum, Newark, New Jersey. Purchased 1937 Felix Fuld Bequest Fund.

This painting has thick, thin, smooth, rough, solid, and broken lines. Where do you see a smooth line? Find a broken line.

Seeing like an artist

Draw different kinds of straight and curved lines. Make them move in different directions.

Lines can be **thick** or **thin**, **smooth** or **rough**, **solid** or **broken**.

Create

How many different kinds of lines do you know? Draw an interesting place using many lines.

1. Think of a place you would like to draw.
2. Draw it using thick, thin, smooth, rough, solid, and broken lines.
3. Paint your picture. Use colors you think describe the feeling of the place.

Erika Price. Age 7. *Seattle.* Oil pastel and watercolor.

Lines Can Show Feelings

Claude Monet. (French). *Poplars on the Epte.* 1891. Tate Gallery, London, England/Art Resource, New York.

This artist used vertical lines for the trees. What kind of line did he use to paint the shoreline? All the lines work together to give a feeling of stillness and quiet.

Seeing like an artist

Think of objects in your neighborhood that look like the lines in Monet's painting.

Artists use **horizontal** and **vertical** lines to give paintings a calm and quiet look.

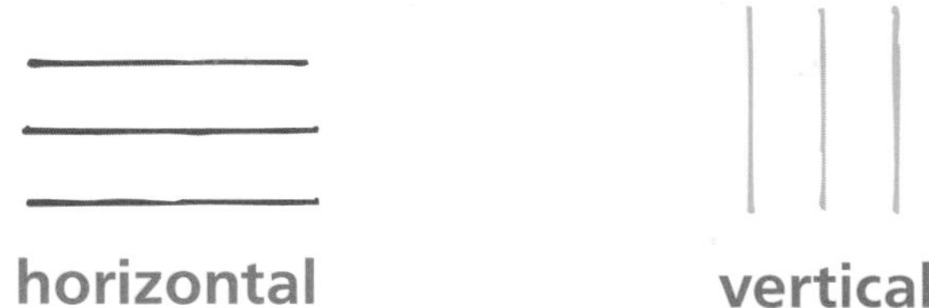

Create

What kinds of lines make things look quiet? Paint a calm place.

1. Think of a calm place. What would you see there?
2. Paint your place. Fill the paper using vertical and horizontal brush strokes.
3. Add details with a marker.

Zach Rearden. Age 7. *Just Like Monet.* Watercolor.

ACTIVE LINES

Wassily Kandinsky. (Russian). *Composition IV.* 1913. Oil on canvas. Hermitage, St. Petersburg, Russia. Scala/Art Resource, New York ©1998 Artists Rights Society, New York. ADAGP, Paris.

Look at the lines in the painting. The artist uses many kinds of lines to show action and add excitement. How do the lines move? Which lines give a feeling of movement?

Seeing like an artist

Think of lines that you could use to describe a birthday party.

Artists use **active lines** to give paintings a feeling of excitement.

diagonal

zigzag

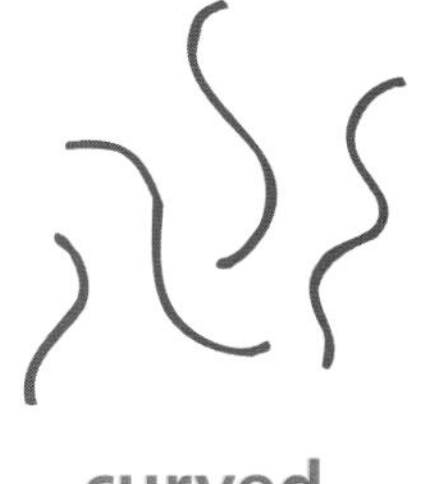

curved

Create

What kinds of lines go with fast music?
Create an active painting.

1. Think about lines to go with your favorite fast music.
2. Draw different active lines with black paint to show the movement of your music.
3. Choose some bright colors and paint all the spaces between the black lines.

Kendall Whittlesey. Age 7. *Kendall's Masterpiece.* Tempera Paint.

Geometric Shapes

Auguste Herbin. (French). *Composition on the Word "Vie" 2.* 1950. Oil on canvas. $57\frac{1}{2} \times 38\frac{1}{4}$ inches. The Museum of Modern Art, New York, New York. The Sidney and Harriet Janis Collection. Photograph ©1998 The Museum of Modern Art, New York./ ©1998 Artists Rights Society (ARS), New York/ADAGP, Paris.

This painting has many shapes. Name all the different shapes you see. Where is the smallest shape? What kind of lines were used to make that shape?

Seeing like an artist

Draw a circle, triangle, or square. Describe the lines you used to make your shape.

Some shapes are geometric.
Geometric shapes have special names.

triangle

square

circle

rectangle

Create

How could you arrange shapes to make a picture? Design a geometric-shape picture.

1. Imagine geometric shapes dancing in the air.
2. Cut out squares, circles, triangles, and rectangles. Cut out different sizes and colors.
3. Arrange the shapes to make a design.

Rebecca Thompson. Age 8. *Robby Robot.* Collage construction paper.

Free-Form Shapes

Artist Unknown. (Indonesia). *Indonesian Shadow Puppet.* c. 1950. Cut, painted leather. $31\frac{1}{2}$ inches high. Private Collection.

Look at this free-form puppet. What kind of shadow do you think it makes? Do you think this puppet would play a friendly or scary part in a play?

Seeing like an artist

Look at shadows of everyday things on a wall. How many can you name from just the shape?

Irregular shapes are **free-form shapes**.
They are not **geometric shapes**.

Create

What kind of shapes could you use to make people and objects? Create a shadow puppet with free-form shapes.

1. Think of a puppet you would like to create.
2. Draw it and cut out the parts.
3. Attach moving parts. Tape the puppet to a stick.
4. Hold the puppet in front of a light to make a shadow.

Ashton Jaska. Age 7. *Cat.* Cut paper.

Lines and Shape in Dance

AMAN International Folk Ensemble: "Suite of French-Canadian Dances." Dancers performing the "Danse des Balais."

These dancers are doing a French-Canadian clog or tap dance. Clogs are shoes with pieces of wood or metal on the bottoms. The dancers clog the rhythm of the dance.

What To Do

Learn a dance.

1. Form a circle. Hold hands.
2. Walk 16 steps to the left. Turn and go 16 steps to the right.
3. Face the center of the circle. Take 4 steps in, then 4 steps back.
4. Take 3 steps in. Bow. Then take 4 steps back.

Extra Credit

Do the dance again, with a small circle inside the big one. Circles can move in the same or opposite directions.

Wrapping Up Unit 1

Line and Shape

Reviewing Main Ideas

Lines are named for the direction in which they move.

- Lines can be thick or thin, smooth or rough, solid or broken.
- Shapes are geometric or free-form.

Suzuki Kiitsu. (Japanese). *Sea Shells and Plums.* Edo Period, nineteenth century. Hanging scroll. Color on silk. $13\frac{5}{8} \times 11$ inches. From the Shin'enkan Collection, Los Angeles County Museum of Art, Los Angeles, California.

Summing Up

Look at the painting. The artist uses many kinds of lines to create shapes and designs.

- Name the kinds of lines you see.
- Tell where you see geometric and free-form shapes.

Artists use lines and shapes to show what they see and how they feel.

Let's Visit a Museum

This museum is in Los Angeles, California. It is made up of five buildings. Inside are more than 100,000 artworks from all over the world. The museum also has two sculpture gardens.

Los Angeles County Museum of Art, Los Angeles, California.

Unit 2

An Introduction to Space and Form

Artist unknown. (Egypt). *The Pyramids at Giza. Mycerinus* (c. 2470 B.C.), *Chefron* (c. 2500 B.C.), and *Cheops* (c. 2530 B.C.). Giza. © Fred J. Maroon/Photo Researchers, Inc.

Shapes have matching forms that have height, width, and depth. Forms take up space and are surrounded by space.

Look at these two pictures.

- What shape matches the forms of these pyramids?
- What form do you see in the Great Sphinx?

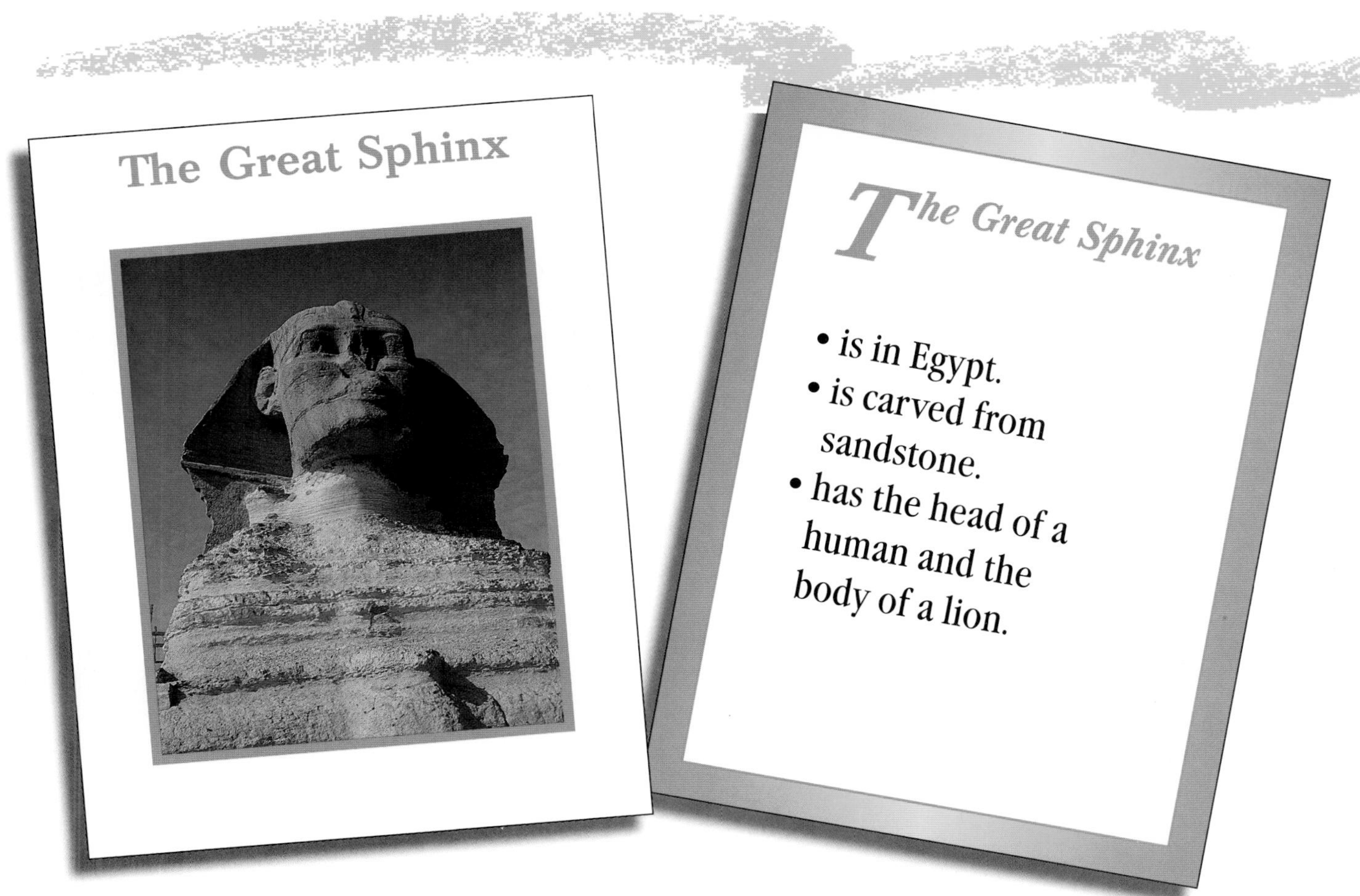

In this unit you will:

- learn how artists use forms and spaces to create depth in their artwork.
- practice using forms and spaces to show depth in your artwork.

Shapes and Forms

Artist unknown. (Italy). *Pantheon.* A.D. 118–128. Concrete, brick, marble, and bronze. 141 feet high. Rome, Italy. Photographer: Louis Grandadam/©Tony Stone Images.

This is a picture of the Pantheon. It shows the height and width of the building shapes. If you saw the Pantheon in person, you would see forms. Forms have height, width, and depth.

Seeing like an artist

Do any neighborhood buildings have the same shapes as the Pantheon?

A dimension is a measurement. Shapes have two dimensions: **height** and **width**. Forms have three dimensions: height, width, and **depth**. Every **two-dimensional** shape has a matching **three-dimensional** (3-D) form.

Create

How would you turn flat shapes into solid forms? Construct a 3-D building.

1. Think about the plans you would draw for a building. Make 3-D paper forms to fit your plans.
2. Combine the forms with slits, tabs, or glue to make your building.
3. Set the form on a piece of cardboard. Draw or construct a setting around the building.

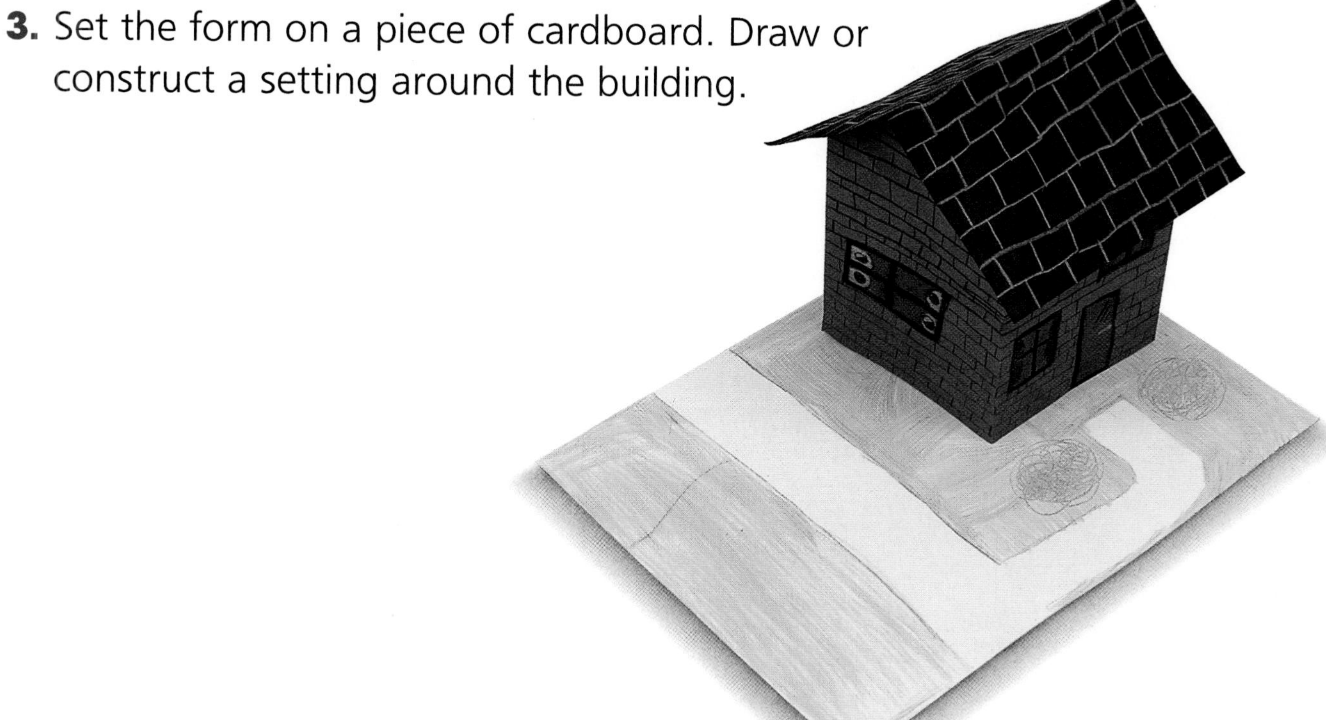

Hannah Angel. Age 8. *My House.* Construction paper.

Face Forms

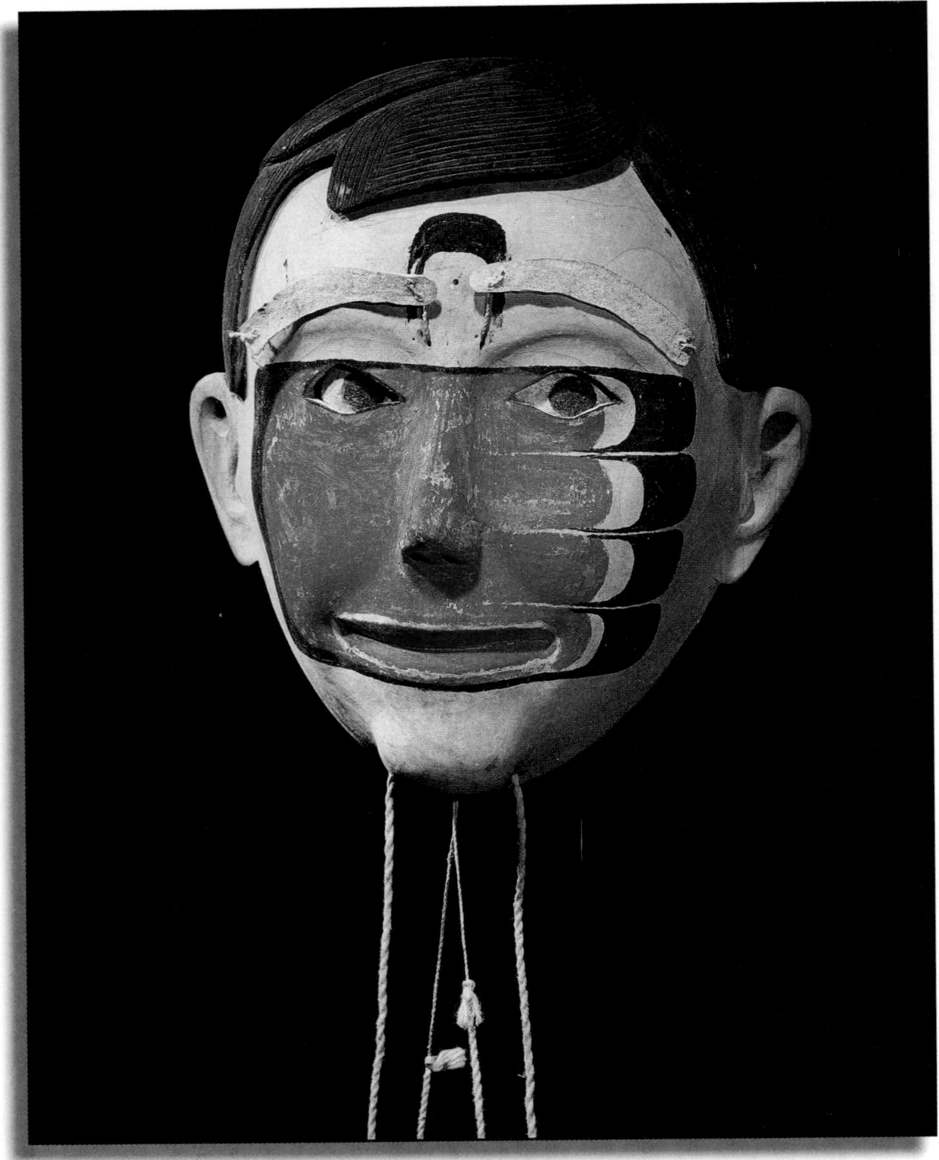

Artist unknown. (North America). *Self-Portrait Mask.* Pre-1900. Carved wood, string, and skin. Courtesy of the Royal British Columbia Museum, Victoria, British Columbia, Cananda. #10665.

Native American masks are made from natural things like wood, skins, grasses, shells, and fur. Some mask artists use string to make parts move. Which parts of this mask look like they move?

Seeing like an artist

Make faces in a mirror to show strong feelings, like anger. See how your face changes.

The human head is a three-dimensional form. It has **height**, **width**, and **depth**. Depth is deep space.

Create

How do the shapes of your face change when you smile or frown? Make a 3-D mask that shows feelings.

1. Think of how you can make a mask that shows feelings.
2. Cut out a face from a folded piece of paper. Cut along the fold. Overlap and glue to make a 3-D form.
3. Make eyes, nose, hair, eyebrows, and eyelashes. Glue them onto the mask. Add a mouth.

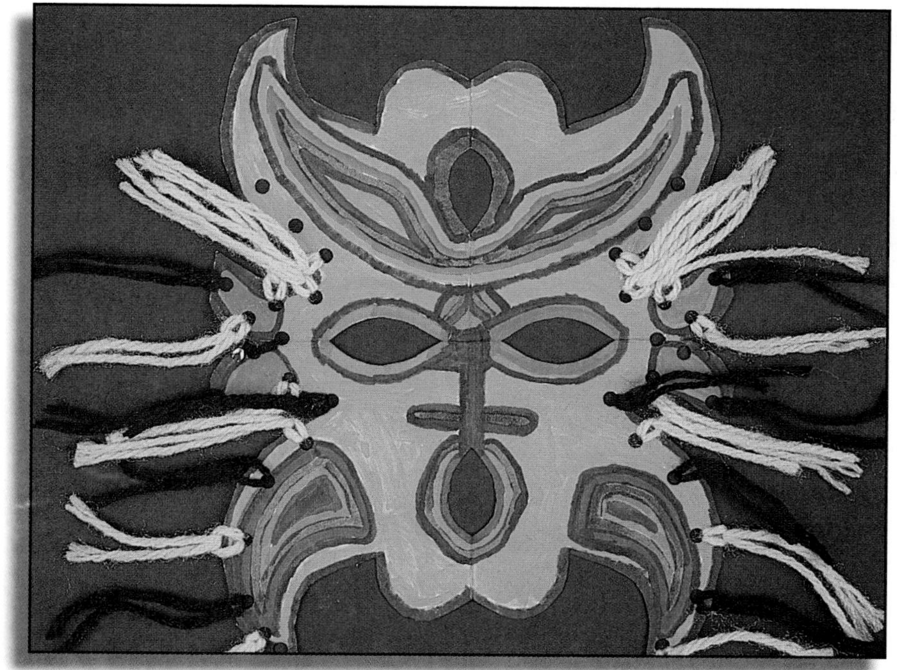

David Compos. Age 8. *Mask.* Marker and yarn.

Body Forms

Roxanne Swentzell. (American). *The Emergence Of The Clowns.* 1988. Coiled and scraped clay. A. 58.4 × 33 × 33 cm; B. 43.2 × 55.9 × 45.7 cm; C. 43.2 × 35.6 × 35.6 cm; D. 17.8 × 43.8 × 26 cm. Heard Museum, Phoenix, Arizona.

An artist made these Pueblo clowns from clay. How many clowns do you see? Are they all the same size? What is each clown doing? Describe the look on each clown's face.

Seeing like an artist

Pretend you are waking up. Stretch while sitting. How does your body move?

People are **free-form, three-dimensional** forms. People take up space.

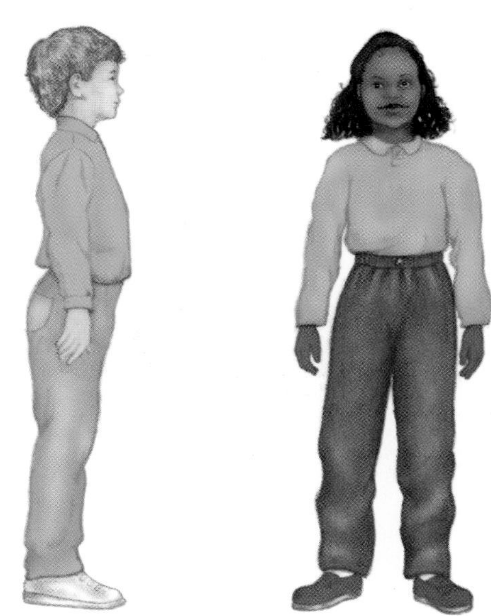

Create

How do the sizes of people differ? Model two or more human forms.

1. Think of the parts of the body. Allow space for them on the clay.
2. Gently squeeze the clay to make a neck.
3. Pull out short arms and legs. Add more clay if needed. Make the figures stand, sit, or lie down.

Sarah Leggett. Age 7.
A Relaxing Afternoon. Clay.

Shapes in Space

James J. Shannon. (American). *Jungle Tales.* 1895. Oil on canvas. $34\frac{1}{4} \times 44\frac{3}{4}$ inches. Metropolitan Museum of Art, New York, New York. Arthur Hoppock Hearn Fund, 1913.

Look at the bodies of the people in this painting. You cannot see all of the girl in the center. Why? Other bodies hide or overlap her body. Overlapping is one way artists show depth.

Seeing like an artist

Put two objects on your desk, one in front of the other. What part of the object in back is hidden by the one in front?

Artists overlap shapes to create **depth**. Depth is deep space.

Create

Why are friends hard to see in crowds? Overlap shapes of people playing.

1. Think about the way you move when you play.
2. Draw five people playing. Cut them out.
3. Arrange and overlap the shapes on white paper. Move them until you like what you see. Glue them onto the paper.

Sarah Hartley. Age 8. *Cheerleading.* Construction paper.

Objects in Space

Paul Cézanne. (French). *Still Life with Apples.* 1895-98. Oil on canvas. 27 × 36½ inches. The Museum of Modern Art, New York, New York. Photograph ©1998 The Museum of Modern Art, New York.

This painting is a still life. A still life is a collection of objects that do not move. Find the overlapping shapes in the painting. Which object looks the closest to you?

Seeing like an artist

Look out a window. Find an object that overlaps something farther away.

We see depth in **still life** pictures when objects in the pictures **overlap**. Depth is deep space.

Create

How would you set up an interesting still life? Arrange and paint a still life using overlapping.

1. Think of some small objects you'd like to draw.
2. Arrange your objects so that some overlap.
3. Use chalk to draw the objects closest to you. Then, draw the objects that have hidden parts.
4. Paint your still life.

Robert Pirkle. Age 8. *Sporting Goods.* Tempera.

Animal Forms

Artist Unknown. (India). *Votive Horse.* Clay. From the Girard Foundation Collection, in the Museum of International Folk Art, a unit of the Museum of New Mexico, Santa Fe, New Mexico. Photographer: Michel Monteaux.

Look at the legs on this clay horse. Two are side by side in front, and two are side by side in back. If you saw the horse from the back, would it look the same?

Seeing like an artist

Look at pictures of animals. What makes one kind of animal look different from another?

Animals are 3-D forms. They have **height**, **width**, and **depth**. Animals take up space.

Create

What animals do you think have the most interesting shapes? Create a four-legged animal.

1. Think of an animal you'd like to make with clay. Gently squeeze a neck to separate the head and body.
2. Pull legs from the body. Show an animal standing or moving.
3. Add details by pulling or blending clay.

Sarah Bargeron. Age 8.
Little Giraffe. Earthenware clay.

Forms and Space in Acting

David Novak, storyteller.

David Novak acts out well-known stories and poems. He clowns, juggles, and uses puppets. He gets the audience involved in his shows. As he moves, David changes the space around him.

What To Do

Make a storyboard.

1. Choose a favorite story. Talk about what happened at the beginning, the middle, and the end.
2. Draw something important that happened in the story.
3. Put all the drawings in order to show what happened.
4. Draw any missing events. Put them with the other drawings.
5. Take turns retelling parts of the story.

Extra Credit

Storyboard another story. Use your drawings to retell the story to the class.

Wrapping Up Unit 2

Space and Form

Reviewing Main Ideas

Every flat, 2-D shape has a matching 3-D form.

- Forms have height, width, and depth.
- Artists overlap shapes to create depth.

Barbara Hepworth. (British). *Figure Churinga.* 1952. Spanish mahogany. $47\frac{7}{16} \times 12\frac{1}{4} \times 12\frac{15}{16}$ inches. Collection Walker Art Center, Minneapolis, Minnesota. Gift of the T.B. Walker Foundation, 1955.

Careers in Art

Barbara Hepworth was a sculptor. She lived in England. She made sculptures from stone, wood, and bronze. She earned her living as an artist.

Summing Up

Look at the sculpture. The artist used form and space in her artwork.

- Does the sculpture remind you of anything? What?
- How does the hole in the sculpture change the space around the form?

Artists arrange shapes and forms to show space and depth.

Barbara Hepworth, sculptor

Unit 3

An Introduction to Color and Value

Georgia O'Keeffe. (American). *The Red Poppy.* 1927. Oil on canvas. Private collection. Art Resource NY/©1998 The Georgia O'Keeffe Foundation/Artists Rights Society (ARS), New York.

Value is the lightness or darkness of a color.

This artist used colors and values.

- What is the most important color in the painting?
- Tell where a color changes value to become lighter or darker.

Artist Profile

In this unit you will:

- learn how artists mix colors and use values in their artwork.
- practice using colors and values in your artwork.

Rainbow Colors

Robert Lostutter. (American). *Baird Trogon.* 1985. Watercolor over graphite on paper. $24\frac{1}{4} \times 34\frac{5}{8}$ inches. Art Institute of Chicago, Chicago, Illinois. Restricted Gift of the Illinois Arts Council, Logan Fund, 1985.348.

To make this picture, the artist first drew the face with a pencil. Then he painted over the lines. What colors do you see? Describe the textures of the face and feathers.

Seeing like an artist

Vote for your favorite color. Your classmates will vote, too. Which color is most popular?

Red, blue, and yellow are **primary hues**, or colors. Two primary hues can be mixed to make a **secondary hue**.

Create

Where would you use rainbow colors in your own art? Design a stencil print.

1. Think of a shape you like. Draw it and cut it out.
2. Lay the stencil on paper. Dab paint in the open space.
3. Make more shapes. Use one sponge for each color. Let shapes overlap. What happens?

Lauren Haupt. Age 7. ***Triangle Design.*** Tempera paint.

Light and Dark

Edward J. Steichen. (American). *The Flatiron—Evening.* 1904. Photograph. $18\frac{13}{16} \times 15\frac{1}{8}$ inches. Metropolitan Museum of Art, New York, New York. Alfred Stieglitz Collection, 1933.

A **photographer** uses light and dark to suggest a feeling or mood. Look at the light and dark values in this photo. What mood do these values show?

Seeing like an artist

Pick three objects in your classroom. Draw one black, one white, and one gray.

The lightness or darkness of an object is called its **value**.

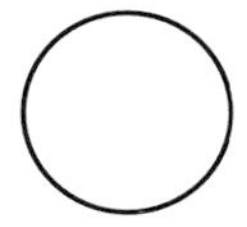
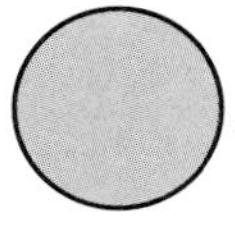

Black + White = Gray

Light Gray (more white)

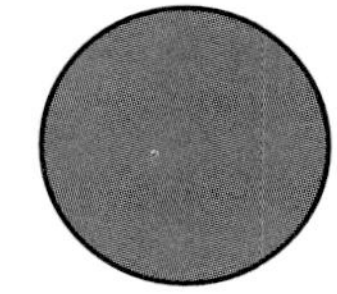

Dark Gray (more black)

Create

Where do you see light and dark values?
Paint a black-and-white picture.

1. Think of a shape you'd like to draw. Paint it white.
2. Mix black and white paint. Make a gray stripe around the white shape.
3. Mix darker values until you get black. Paint a stripe of each value around your shape.

Brian Magelsson. Age 7. *Screen Saver.* Tempera.

Light Values

Jane Wilson. (American). *Solstice.* 1991. Oil on linen. 60 × 70 inches. Courtesy of the Fischbach Gallery, New York, New York.

This artist uses light values in a calm landscape. Describe the colors you see. What **mood** do the light values create? What would you have called the painting?

Seeing like an artist

Look for an object with a light value. Draw and lightly color that object.

Light **values** of **hues** are called **tints**.

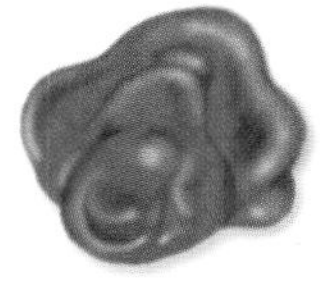

Blue + White

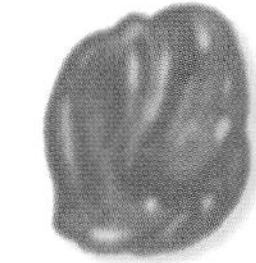

Violet + White

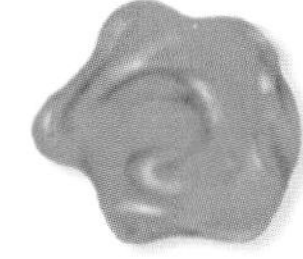

Green + White

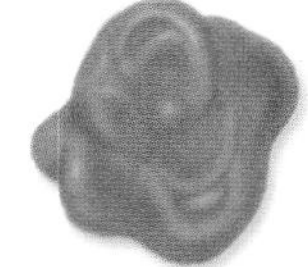

Red + White

Yellow + White

Orange + White

Create

Where would you use tints in a foggy landscape painting? Create a mood picture.

1. Think of three colors to use.
2. Add small amounts of each color to white to make tints.
3. Fill your paper with a scene about a foggy day.

Jessie Little. Age 6. *The Pink Tree.* Tempera.

Dark Values

Adolph Gottlieb. (American). *Spectre of the Sea.* 1947. Oil on canvas. 30 × 38 inches. The Montclair Art Museum, Montclair, New Jersey. © 1998 Adolph and Esther Gottlieb Foundation/Licensed by VAGA, New York, NY.

This artist painted lines and shapes with dark values. Describe the colors you see in the painting. What is the mood? What do you think the painting is about?

Seeing like an artist

Darken your classroom. Draw a familiar object as it looks in the dark.

Dark values of **hues** are called **shades**.

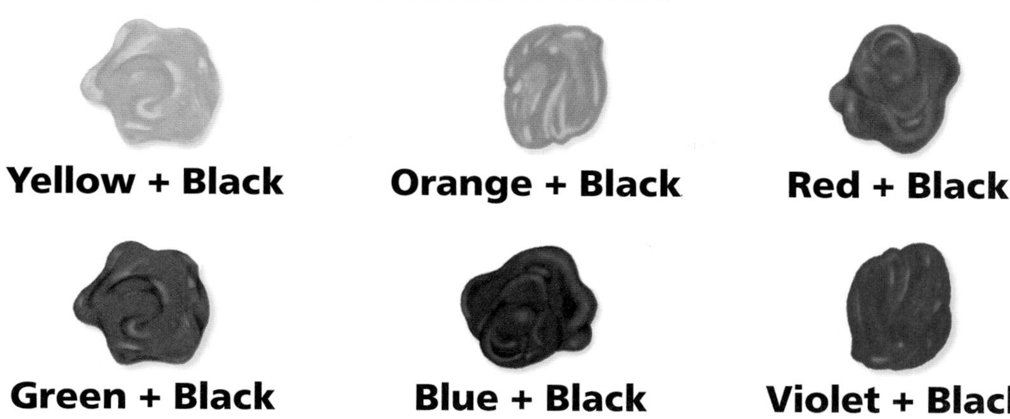

Create

How would you use shades in your artwork? Draw a night scene or a dark, rainy day scene.

1. Think of three colors to use.
2. Mix a small amount of black with each color.
3. Paint a picture of a dark scene with the three shades.

Lorenzo Lopez. Age 7. *Rainy and Dreary Day.* Tempera.

Warm and Cool Hues

Patrick Des Jarlait. (American). *Gathering Wild Rice.* 1972. Watercolor on paper. 27.8 × 39.5 cm. Heard Museum, Phoenix, Arizona.

Notice the yellows, oranges, and reds in this painting. These are warm colors. Who in the painting is gathering rice? Describe the mood or feeling of the painting.

Seeing like an artist

Look around your classroom. Name things that have warm colors.

Red, yellow, and orange are **warm hues**. Blue, green, and violet are **cool hues**.

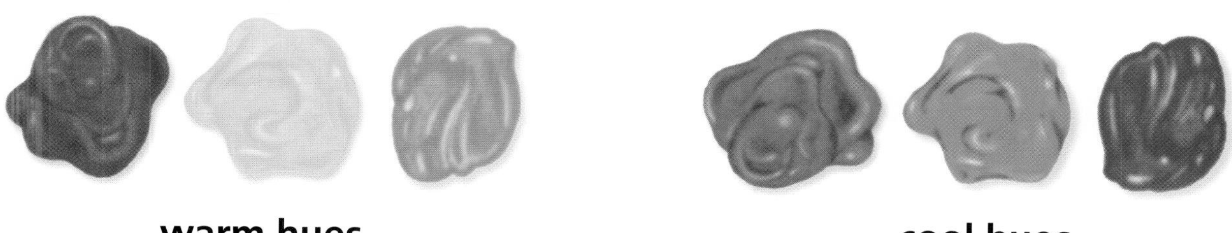

warm hues

cool hues

Create

Where do you see warm and cool hues? Draw a design.

1. Think of a circle. Draw it with an oil pastel. Print your first name inside the circle.
2. Draw lines to connect the letters and the circle.
3. Paint the spaces with warm or cool colors.

Sean Scott. Age 8. *The Stained Glass Window.* Tempera and oil pastel.

Warm or Cool Scene?

Tom Thomson. (Canadian). *Spring Ice.* 1916. Oil on canvas. 72 × 102.3 cm. National Gallery of Canada, Ottawa, Ontario, Canada.

This painting shows a cold spring day in Canada. Melting ice floats on the water. Describe the colors and **mood**. Does the painting remind you of a place you know?

Seeing like an artist

What plants and animals would you find in a place that is cold all year?

Blue, green, and purple are **cool colors**.

  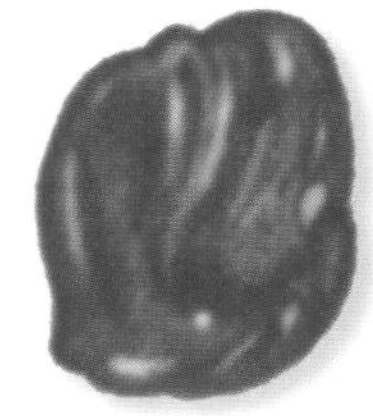

Create

How do paintings with cool colors make you feel? Create a landscape.

1. Imagine the outdoors. Tear paper to make stencils of hills and mountains.
2. Rub chalk over the stencils' edges onto paper. Brush with a tissue.
3. Overlap shapes. Fill your paper.

Madison Meyer. Age 8. *Mountains.* Chalk.

The Color of Music

Arco Iris: Danais Tokatlian and Ara Tokatlian, musicians.

Arco Iris musicians play traditional music of the Americas. Sometimes they use a bombo legüero, or hollow log drum, from Argentina. They also play modern instruments like saxophones and electric guitars.

What To Do

Learn an easy-to-sing song.

1. Sing the first two parts of the song. Your teacher will sing part three.
2. Sing the whole song.
3. Work with a group. Sing different parts. Tap the beats as you sing.

Extra Credit

Use a drum, wood block, tambourine, or shaker to play the rhythm as you sing.

Wrapping Up Unit 3

Color and Value

Reviewing Main Ideas

Hue is another name for color.

- Red, blue, and yellow are primary hues.
- Orange, green, and violet are secondary hues.
- Value is the lightness or darkness of a color. Tints are light values. Shades are dark values.
- Warm colors are red, orange, and yellow.
- Cool colors are green, blue, and violet.

George Bellows. (American). *Portrait of Anne.* 1915. Oil on canvas. $48\frac{1}{8} \times 36\frac{1}{4}$ inches. Collection of the High Museum of Art, Atlanta, Georgia. Purchase with Henry B. Scott Fund.

Let's Visit a Museum

This museum is in Atlanta, Georgia. It has more than 10,000 works of art from all over the world. The museum's building has won awards because of its beautiful architecture.

Summing Up

Look at the portrait. The colors create a mood.

- What primary colors do you see?
- Find the tints and shades.
- What cool colors do you see?

Artists use colors, tints, and shades to control the mood in the work.

The High Museum of Art, Atlanta, Georgia.

Unit 4

An Introduction to Movement and Rhythm

Louise Nevelson. (American). *Dawn.* 1962. Gold painted wood. $94\frac{1}{2} \times 75\frac{1}{2} \times 7\frac{3}{4}$ inches. The Pace Wildenstein Gallery, New York, New York.

Repeating colors, shapes, or lines creates a pattern or rhythm. Artists use patterns and lines to make our eyes move around their artwork.

Look at this sculpture.

- What shapes are repeated?
- What kinds of lines lead your eyes through the artwork?

Artist Profile

In this unit you will:

- learn how artists create rhythms and visual movement in their artwork.
- practice creating rhythms and visual movement in your artwork.

Diagonal Movement

Thomas Hart Benton. (American). *I Got a Girl on Sourwood Mountain.* 1938. Lithograph. $12\frac{1}{2} \times 9\frac{1}{4}$ inches. Reproduced from the collections of the Library of Congress, Washington, DC.

This artist wants us to feel the excitement of music and dancing. He uses diagonal and zigzag lines to make our eyes move around the picture. Can you feel the excitement?

Seeing like an artist

Name times when people's arms and legs move diagonally.

Artists use **diagonal** and **zigzag** lines to create **visual movement**. They make your eyes move through a work of art.

Create

How could you show movement on paper? Draw an active scene.

1. Think about how your arms and legs move.
2. Draw a scene full of movement. Show many people moving. Use slanted and zigzag lines.

Mateo Armas. Age 8. *Surfing*. Marker.

Curving Movement

Vincent van Gogh. (Dutch). *The Starry Night.* 1889. Oil on canvas. 73.7 × 92.1 cm. The Museum of Modern Art, New York, New York. Acquired through the Lillie P. Bliss Bequest. Photograph © 1998 The Museum of Modern Art, New York.

This artist uses curving and swirling lines to create movement in his painting. What colors do you see? Where are the curving lines? Do you see other kinds of lines?

Seeing like an artist

Draw a line in the air that reminds you of big ocean waves.

Artists use **curving** and **swirling lines** to lead your eyes through a painting. These lines can also create movement in the picture itself.

Create

What does it feel like to be surrounded by many moving things? Paint an exciting picture.

1. Think of a place that is full of movement.
2. Draw this place using curving and swirling lines.
3. Paint your place with watercolors.

Dalia Castillo. Age 8. *Amusement Park.* Crayon and watercolor.

Making Designs

Artist unknown. Delaware Tribe (United States). *Delaware Shoulder Bag.* c. 1860. Wool and cotton fabric. 21.9 × 19.7 cm. Detroit Institute of Arts, Detroit, Michigan. Photograph ©1996 Detroit Institute of Arts, Founders Society Purchase.

A repeated motif gives a design its pattern. What colors and shapes are in this design? Do you think this is for everyday wear or for special occasions?

Seeing like an artist

Look for a motif in your clothes and see how it is repeated.

Repeating a **motif** creates **visual rhythms**, or patterns.

Create

Where do you see patterns?
Design a motif.

1. Think of a motif.
   Draw it and cut it out of a sponge.
2. Dip your sponge into paint.
   Make prints on paper.
3. Fill the paper with colors.

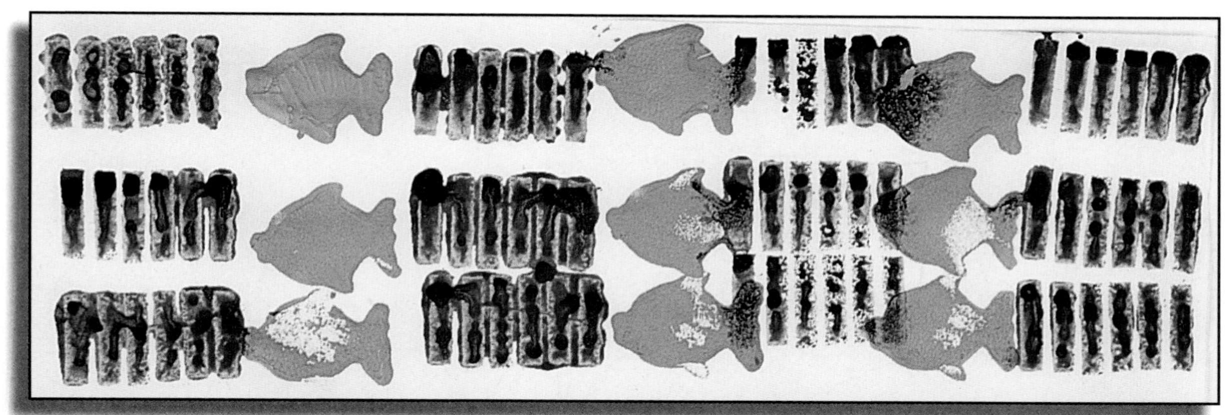

Ronnie McCullough. Age 8. *Fish on a line.* Tempera and sponge.

Floral Designs

Peggy Flora Zalucha. (American). *Peony Blooms (IX).* 1992. Watercolor on paper. 44 × 68 inches. Courtesy of Peggy Flora Zalucha.

Some motifs are repeated in paintings. Describe the colors and repeated motifs in this artwork.

Seeing like an artist

Look around at home. Find two flowers with different patterns.

Repeating a **motif** creates **visual movement** and **rhythm**.

Create

Where do you see rhythm in nature? Design a floral motif.

1. Think of a motif. Draw it on a paper circle.
2. With a pencil point, carve the design on a Styrofoam circle.
3. Roll ink evenly over the motif. Print it on a paper strip. Make more prints.

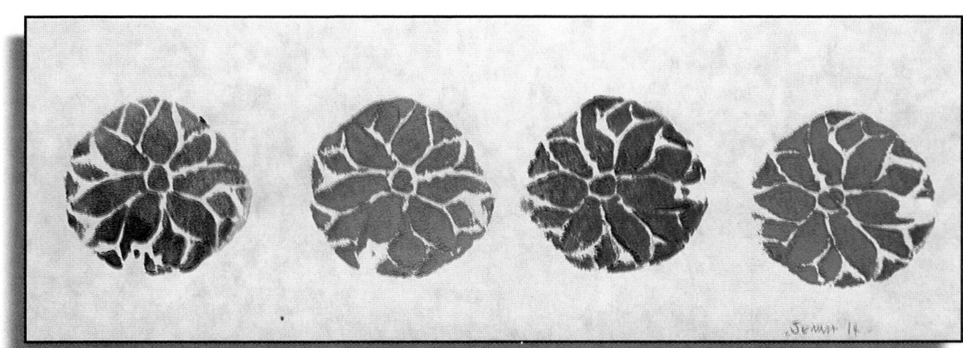

Jenna Hershey. Age 8. *Flowers.* Styrofoam stamp with tempera.

Showing Patterns

Suad al-Attar. (Iraqi). *Untitled/Iraq.* 1981. Lithograph on paper. $29\frac{1}{2} \times 22\frac{1}{2}$ inches. The National Museum of Women in the Arts, Washington, DC. Gift of Wedad and Adel Almandil.

This artist drew patterns she saw in flowers and birds. What patterns do you see? Why do you think she made a tree in the shape of a circle?

Seeing like an artist

When you're outside, what patterns do you see in plants and animals?

Many objects in nature have **rhythm**, or patterns.

Create

What kinds of patterns have you seen around you? Draw a natural object that has patterns.

1. Think of an animal or plant. Draw it large.
2. Add lines and shapes to make natural patterns.
3. Redraw your lines with glue to add texture. Let the drawing dry. Fill in the shapes.

Belinda Rivera. Age 8. *Flower.* Oil pastel.

Showing Collections

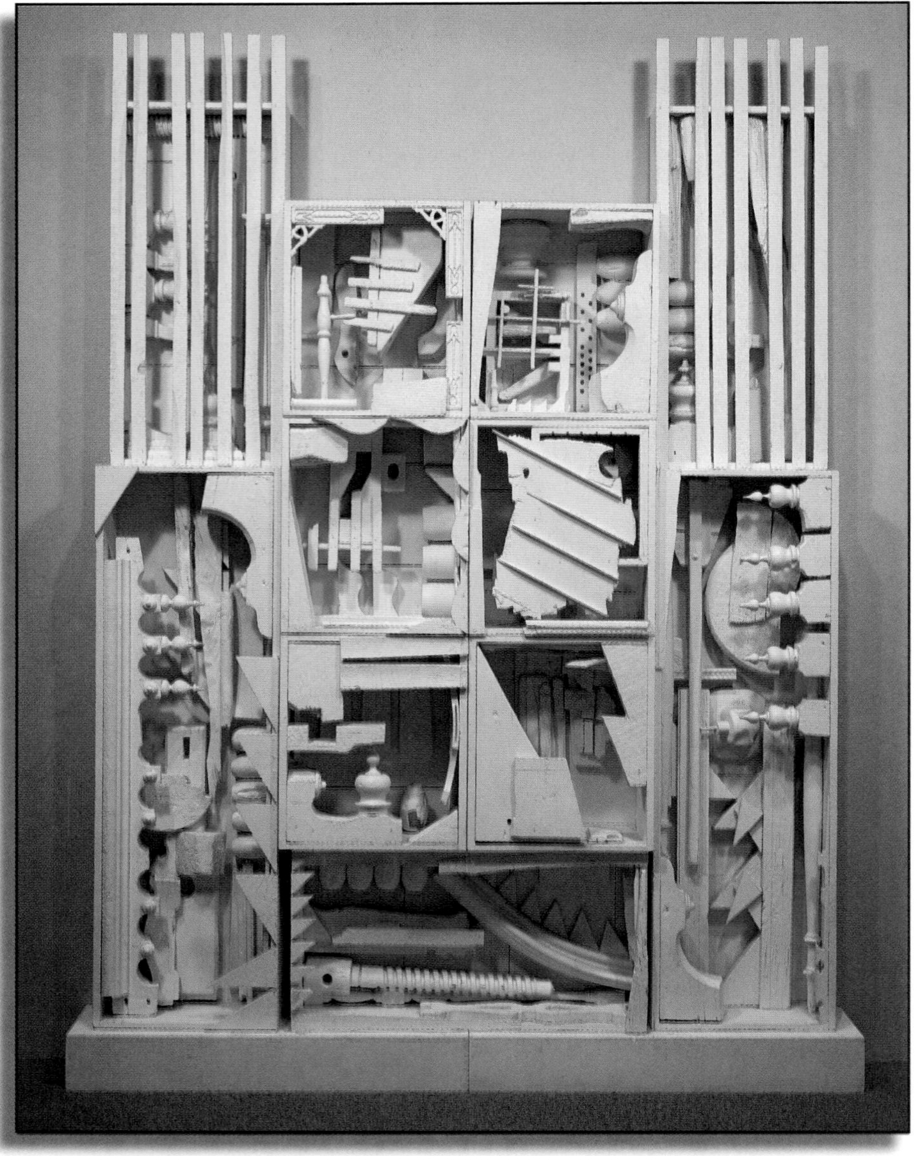

Louise Nevelson. (American). *Dawn's Wedding Chapel II.* 1959. White painted wood. $115\frac{7}{8} \times 83\frac{1}{2} \times 10\frac{1}{2}$ inches. Collection of Whitney Museum of American Art, New York, New York. Purchased with funds from the Howard and Jean Lipman Foundation, Inc.

This sculptor uses wood scraps to show an idea. Describe the objects in her **sculpture.** What do the objects make you think of?

Seeing like an artist

How would you arrange a collection of your things to make a pattern?

Artists can create **visual patterns** by arranging found objects.

Create

How can you arrange objects to make a pattern? Design a sculpture.

1. Think of objects you would like to use.
2. Glue paper strips to divide a box into sections. Arrange and glue objects in each section to create patterns.
3. Display all the boxes your class made.

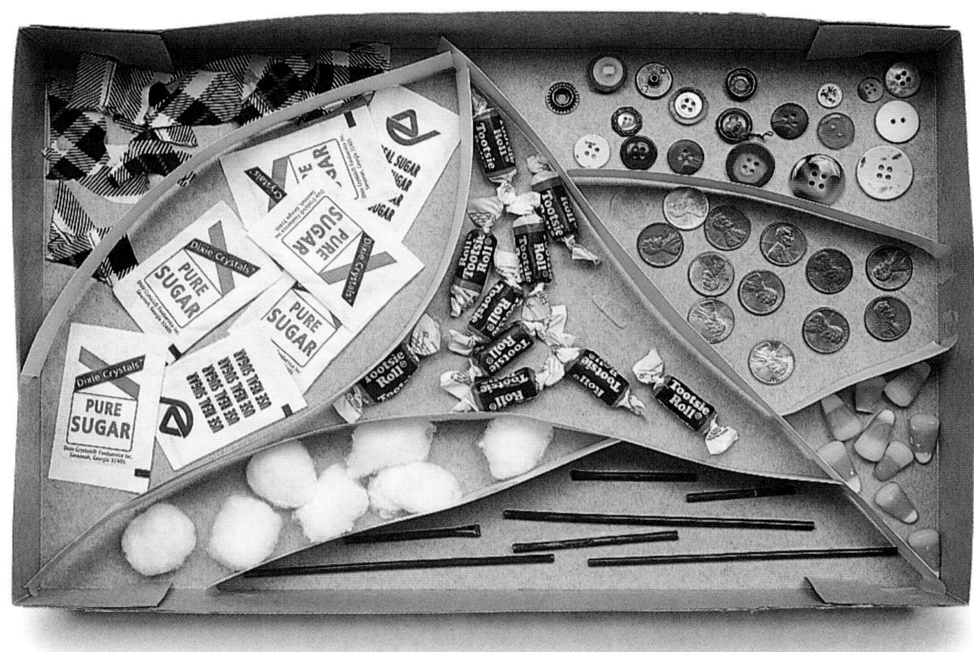

Jim Sirani. Age 8. *Collection Box*. Mixed media.

Rhythm in Sounds

The Robert Minden Ensemble: Sketch of the musicians and the instruments they play.

The Robert Minden Ensemble uses ordinary things to tell musical stories. For one story, the group uses a saw, wood, cans, vacuum cleaner hoses, a Slinky, sea shells, and an underwater phone.

What To Do

Listen to and describe ordinary sounds in your environment.

1. Close your eyes. Listen to the sounds in your classroom.
2. Write some words that describe what you hear when your room is quiet.
3. Take turns reading your descriptions. Did everyone hear the same sounds?

Extra Credit

Listen again, but at a different time of day. Are the sounds the same or different?

Wrapping Up Unit 4

Movement and Rhythm

Reviewing Main Ideas

Artists create visual movement and rhythm in their artwork.

- Rhythm is created by repeating lines, shapes, colors, or textures.
- Visual movement leads your eyes through a work of art.
- A motif is a pattern that is repeated in an artwork.

Max Weber. (American). *Chinese Restaurant.* 1915. Oil on canvas. 40 × 48 inches. Collection of the Whitney Museum of American Art, New York, New York.

Careers in Art

I.M. Pei

is an architect who lives in New York. He designs buildings all over the world. His buildings are very different from each other.

Summing Up

Look at the painting. The artist shows the light, color, and movement of a restaurant.

- Find the visual rhythms. Where do you see color rhythms, shape rhythms, and lines?
- Name one motif. Explain how it is repeated.

Artists use rhythm and movement to create a mood.

I.M. Pei, Architect

Unit 5

An Introduction to Balance, Texture, and Emphasis

Rembrandt van Rijn. (Dutch). *The Return of the Prodigal Son.* c. 1665. Oil on canvas. The Hermitage, St. Petersburg, Russia, Scala, Art Resource, NY.

Artists emphasize, or stress, the most important part of their work. Texture may be used to emphasize artwork.

- What objects in this painting look more important?
- How do you think the clothing in the painting would feel if you touched it?

Artist Profile

Self-Portrait.

In this unit you will:

- learn how artists use balance, texture, and emphasis in their artwork.
- practice using balance, texture, and emphasis in your artwork.

Unit 5 Lesson 1

Formal Balance

Artist unknown. (China). *Gui Ritual Food Container (Zhou Dynasty)*. Eleventh century B.C. Bronze. Courtesy of the Arthur M. Sackler Gallery, Smithsonian Institution, Washington, DC.

Look at this Chinese jar. Trace its **shape** with your finger. Is the shape the same on both sides? That is because the jar has balance.

Seeing like an artist

Look for an object that has balance. Draw a picture of it.

An object has **formal balance** when both halves are the same.

Create

How could you give a jar formal balance? Design a symmetrical jar.

1. Think about the jar you want to make.
2. Fold paper in half. Draw and cut out your jar shape.
3. Cut out small matching shapes.
   Glue the shapes onto the jar using formal balance.

Amber Mooney. Age 8. *The Magic Pot.* Cut paper.

Formal Balance in Bodies

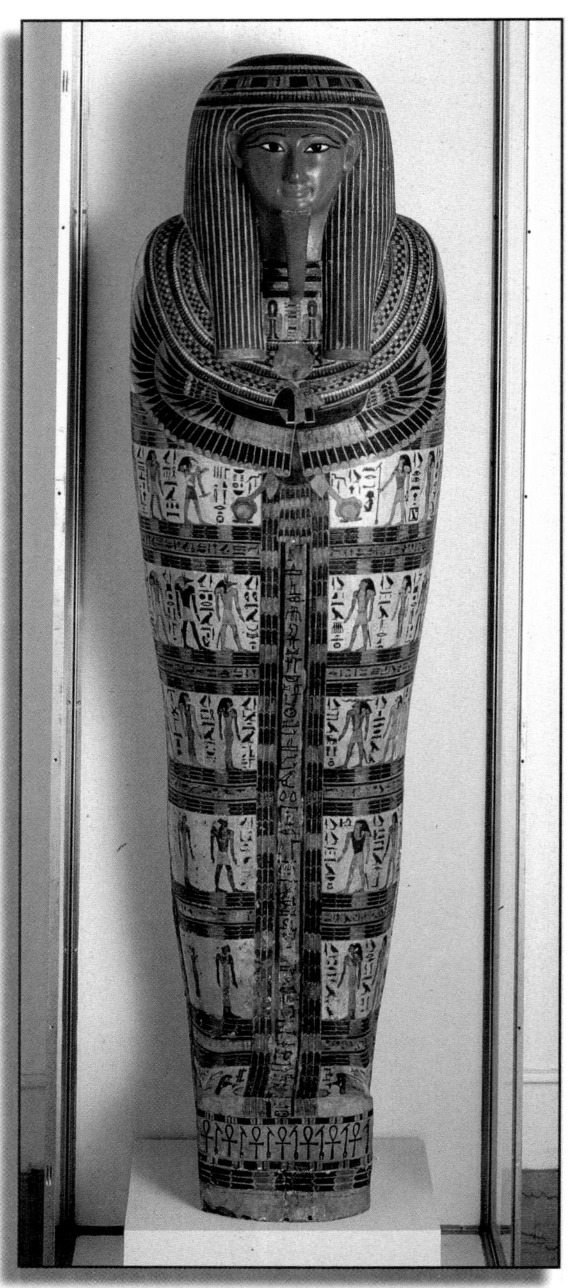

Artist unknown. (Egypt). *Egyptian Mummy Case. c. 945–715 B.C.* Wood. The Brooklyn Museum, New York, New York.

A mummy case is called a **sarcophagus**. It is made to hold a human body. The body has balance. The shape of the case does, too. Are the case designs symmetrical?

Seeing like an artist

Think of a friend. What makes his or her body symmetrical?

Many things in nature have **formal balance**, or **symmetry**.

Create

What kinds of designs would you use to create formal balance in a mummy case? Design a "royal" mummy case.

1. Think about a mummy case.
2. Fold paper in half, then open it. Let someone lie on the fold, arms across his or her chest. Draw around the person's body. Cut it out.
3. Draw symmetrical designs and paint the case.

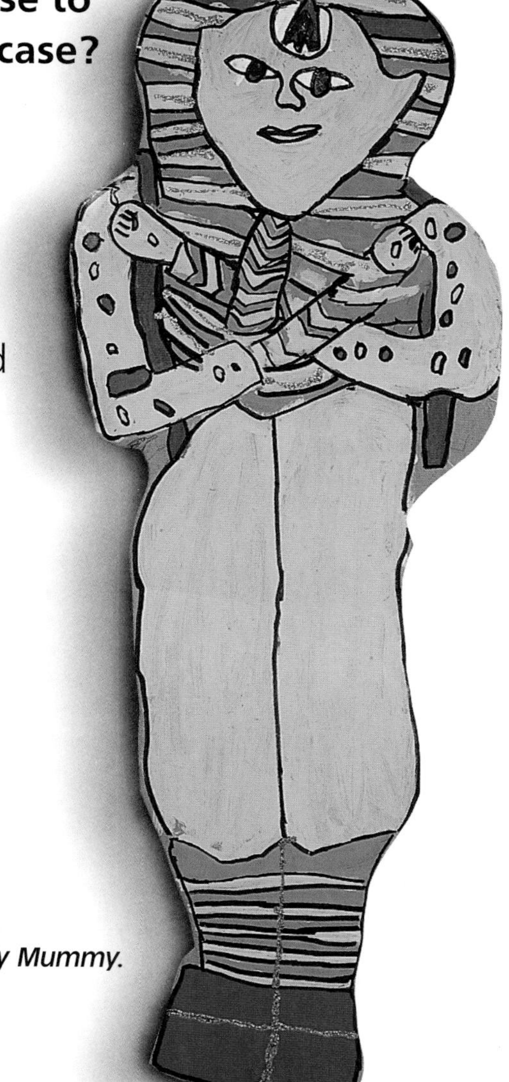

Victor Villegas. Age 9. *My Mummy.* Tempera.

Formal Balance in Furniture

Thomas Affleck. (American). *Side Chair.* 1770. Mahogany, white cedar, 20th century silk damask upholstery. $36\frac{7}{8} \times 21\frac{7}{8} \times 18\frac{3}{8}$ inches. Philadelphia Museum of Art, Philadelphia, Pennsylvania. Gift of Robert L. McNeil, Jr.

Furniture should be symmetrical. Why? Because our bodies are symmetrical. Look at this chair. Is it symmetrical? Do you think it would be comfortable?

Seeing like an artist

Is every chair in your room the same size and shape? Which is most comfortable?

Furniture has **formal balance**. It is built to match the formal balance of our bodies.

Create

What shape would you choose for a furniture design? Design a model chair or sofa.

1. Think about the chair or sofa you want to make.
2. Cut out a seat, sides, arms, legs, and a back. Make tabs on each one. Cut slits for the tabs to go into.
3. Construct a symmetrical model. Fold legs to glue on. Paint the model.

Calvin Cresting. Age 8. *Sitting.* Tempera and cut paper.

Tactile Texture

Harriet Powers. (American). *Pictorial Quilt (detail: Falling Stars 1894–95).* 1895–98. Pieced and appliqued cotton embroidered with plain and metallic yarns, 69 × 105 inches. The Museum of Fine Arts, Boston, Massachusetts. Bequest of Maxim Karolik.

Some artists sew fabric in their work to add texture. This artwork has texture you can see and feel. Describe how you think this quilt would feel.

Seeing like an artist

Imagine your crayon is thread. Draw an object that looks as if you sewed it.

You can feel **tactile texture**. You can see **visual texture**.

visual texture

tactile texture

Create

What kinds of textures would you sew on fabric? Sew a work of art.

1. Think about a design you can make with fabric. Draw your ideas onto fabric scraps.
2. Cut them out and stitch them onto your fabric background.
3. Add more details with stitches and buttons.

Mike Cremeans. Age 8. *Work of Art.* Burlap, yarn, and material.

Texture and Emphasis

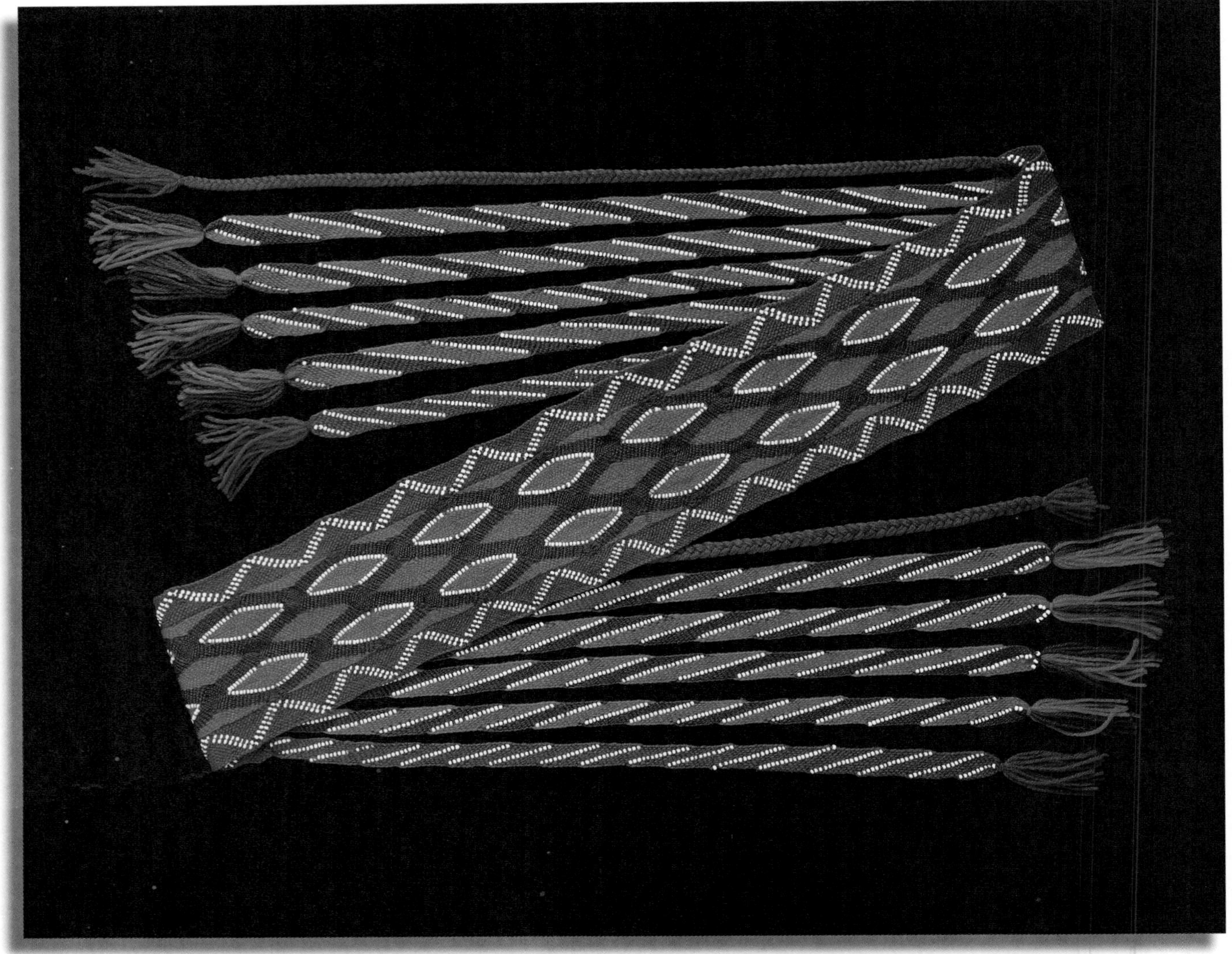

Artist unknown. Osage (United States). *Sash.* 1885.
Wool yarn and glass beads. 213.7 cm. Detroit Institute of Arts, Detroit, Michigan. Photograph ©1996 Detroit Institute of Arts, Founders Society Purchase.

The texture in this fabric can be seen and felt. Describe the colors. Which part of the artwork looks most important? How did the artist emphasize, or stress, that part?

Seeing like an artist

Look closely at the fabrics in your clothes. Describe the textures you see.

Weavers give **emphasis**, or stress, to the most important part of their fabrics. Color, shape, or **textures** make one part stand out.

Create

What would you emphasize in your artwork?
Weave a belt that has color emphasis.

1. Think about a belt design to make.
2. Pull yarn through straws and knot the ends together. Weave yarn over and under the straws.
3. Use color to emphasize one part. Remove the straws and tie both ends of the belt.

Jackie Emmett. Age 7. *Peace Belt.* Yarn.

Masks with Texture

Virginia Caswell. (American). *Bullwinkle of the Sea.* Mixed media. Anchorage Museum of History and Art, Anchorage, Alaska. Exhibit: "Is that you? Is that Me?" Photographed by Chris Arend.

An artist made this symmetrical mask from things in her environment. What kinds of things do you see? What is the mood of the mask? How do you think it is used?

Seeing like an artist

Look around. What interesting materials and objects could you use on a mask?

Artists combine **formal balance** and **tactile texture** to make **masks**.

Create

What objects would you use to give a mask texture? Design a mask.

1. Think about a mask.
2. Fold tagboard in half. Draw half of a head shape at the fold. Cut it out.
3. Glue objects with colors and textures onto the mask.

Tim Westall. Age 8. *Mask.* Marker and yarn.

Emphasis in Music

Korean dancer playing a drum.

Korean folk music has been around for more than 2,000 years. The music may sound different to you. Why? Some Korean songs are made up of only the tones of the black keys on a piano.

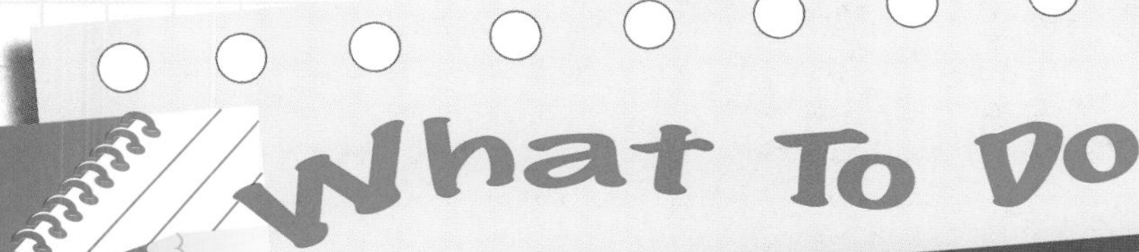

Listen to a Korean song and create a dance to go with it.

1. Listen to the music.
   Tap the beat.
2. Sway back and forth.
   Feel the rhythm of the music.
3. Work with a partner.
   Make up a dance.
   Perform it for the class.

Extra Credit

Use a drum or tambourine to emphasize, or accent, the strong beats in the song.

Balance, Texture, and Emphasis

Reviewing Main Ideas

Artists use balance, texture, and emphasis in their artwork.

- Formal balance means both halves of an object are the same.
- You can see and feel tactile texture. You can see visual texture but cannot feel it.
- Emphasis makes one part of a work of art look more important than the other parts.

Gilbert Stuart. (American). *George Washington. c. 1797*. Oil on canvas. 96 × 60 inches. National Portrait Gallery, Smithsonian Institution, Washington, DC. Anonymous loan. Art Resource, NY.

Let's Visit a Museum

The White House is the home of the President. It is also an art museum. The White House has artwork by America's finest artists.

Summing Up

Look at the painting.

- What textures did the artist show in the painting?
- Does the portrait have formal balance? Explain.
- Which part of the painting did the artist emphasize? How?

The White House, Washington, DC.

Unit 6

An Introduction to

Harmony, Variety, and Unity

Artist unknown. (China). *Sakyamudi Buddha.* A.D. 338. Gilt bronze. $15\frac{1}{2}$ inches high, $9\frac{3}{4}$ inches wide. Asian Art Museum of San Francisco/The Avery Brundage Collection ©1994.
Artist unknown. (Gandhara, Pakistan). *Seated Buddha.* Third century A.D. Schist. $12\frac{3}{4}$ inches high, $8\frac{7}{8}$ inches wide. Asian Art Museum of San Francisco/The Avery Brundage Collection.

For variety, artists add something different to artwork. They use similar things for harmony. If everything goes well together, the artwork has unity.

Look at these three statues of Buddha.

- What is the same about the statues? What is different?
- Does everything in each Buddha design go together?

Artist Profile

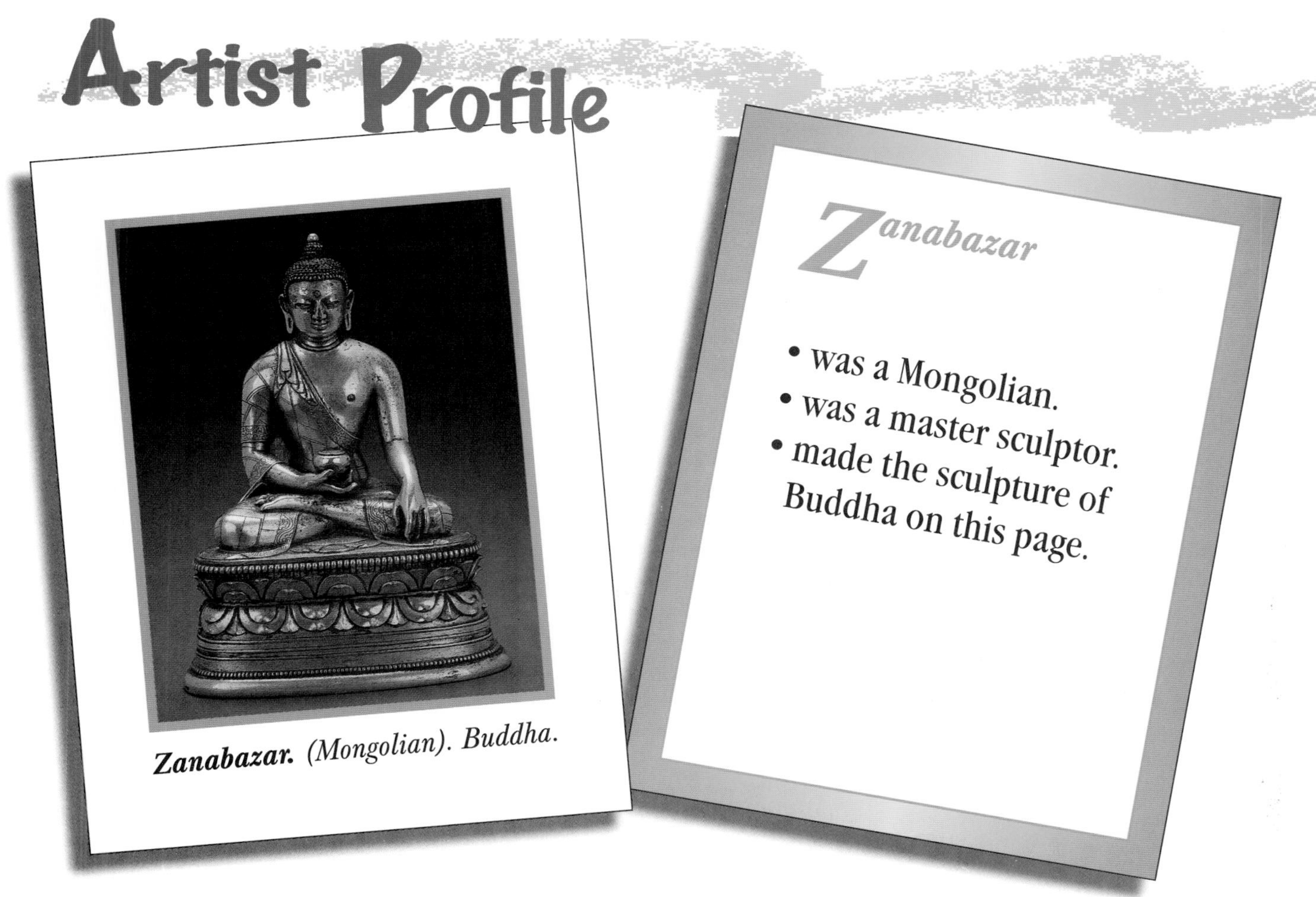

Zanabazar. *(Mongolian). Buddha.*

Zanabazar

- was a Mongolian.
- was a master sculptor.
- made the sculpture of Buddha on this page.

In this unit you will:

- learn how artists use harmony and variety to create unity in their artwork.
- practice using harmony and variety to create unity in your artwork.

Unit 6 Lesson 1

Harmony

Paul Klee. (Swiss). *The Tree of Houses.* 1918. Watercolor and ink on chalk-primed gauze on papers, mounted on painted board. Norton Simon Museum, Pasadena, California. The Blue Four Galka Scheyer Collection, 1953.

Look at this painting. Which shapes are the same? Are any colors alike? Find the ladder at the bottom of the painting. Where do you see the ladder again?

Seeing like an artist

What lines and shapes could represent an animal or a plant you like?

Artists create **harmony**, or a pleasing relationship, by repeating similar parts in artwork.

Create

How can you make different shapes go well together in an artwork? Design a harmonious picture.

1. Think about what kind of design you want to make.
2. Cut out different shapes from related colors, like red and orange or blue and green.
3. Arrange and glue the shapes onto paper. Fill your page.

Kevin Lovett. Age 7. *Weird Shapes.* Cut paper.

Variety

Romare Bearden. (American). *Return of the Prodigal Son.* 1967. Mixed media and collage on canvas. $50\frac{1}{4} \times 60$ inches. Albright Knox Art Gallery, Buffalo, New York. Gift of Mr. and Mrs. Armand J. Castellani, 1981. © 1998 Romare Bearden Foundation/Licensed by VAGA, New York, NY.

This artist uses photos, papers, **fabrics**, paints, and pastels in a **collage**. What shapes, colors, and textures do you see? How many people do you see?

Seeing like an artist

What materials could you use to show an animal, a person, or an object you like?

The use of different lines, shapes, and colors in artwork is called **variety**. Variety makes artwork interesting.

Create

What colors and shapes would you want to use in a collage? Design a collage with variety.

1. Think about lines, shapes, and colors for your collage.
2. Choose some magazine pages. Then, cut out shapes for objects, animals, or people.
3. Arrange and glue the shapes onto paper. Add smaller shapes for details.

Jenny Holzer. Age 7. *Aerial View Landscape.* Old magazines.

Variety and Contrast

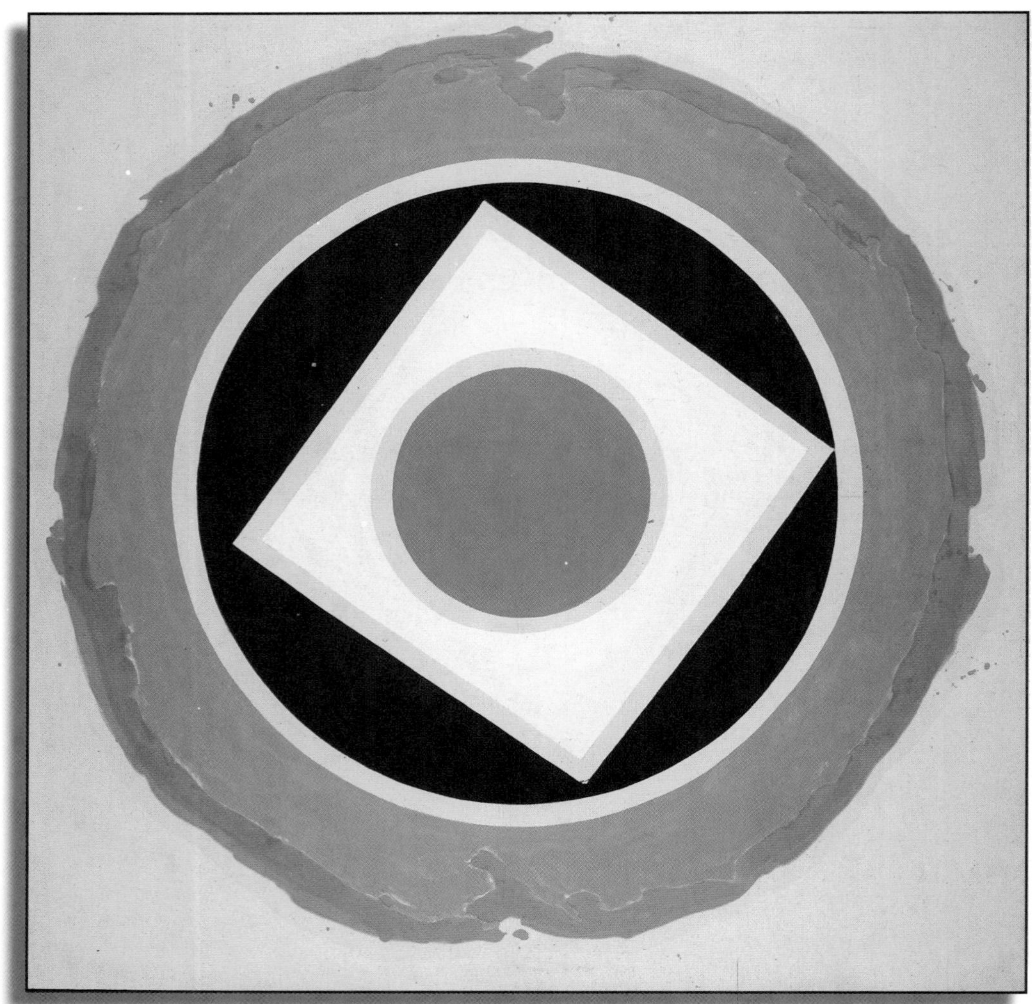

Kenneth Noland. (American). *Split.* 1959. Acrylic on canvas. $94 \times 94\frac{1}{4}$ inches. National Museum of American Art, Smithsonian Institution, Washington, DC. Art Resource, New York. © 1998 Kenneth Noland/Licensed by Vaga, New York, New York.

This artist uses circles of different sizes and colors. Then he adds one more shape. What shape did he add? Does the painting remind you of anything you know?

Seeing like an artist

Find an object with a smooth edge. How would it look with rough edges?

Artists create **variety** in artwork by using **contrast** in colors or shapes.

Create

What shapes and colors would you use to show variety? Design a paper artwork that has variety.

1. Think about warm and cool colors.
2. Cut out one shape in different sizes from warm or cool colors. Glue them onto paper.
3. Tear a different shape so its edges are different, too.

Krista Morman. Age 7. *Shape and Tear.* Cut paper.

Harmony and Unity of Colors

Ivan Eyre. (Canadian). *Touchwood Hills.* 1972–73. Acrylic on canvas. 147.3 × 167.6 cm. National Gallery of Canada, Ottawa, Ontario, Canada.

Look at the different cool colors in this landscape. The similar colors pull everything in the scene together. Does this look like a place you would like to be?

Seeing like an artist

Find an object with colors that are close on a color wheel. What are the colors?

Colors that are close together on a **color wheel** are called **harmonious** colors.

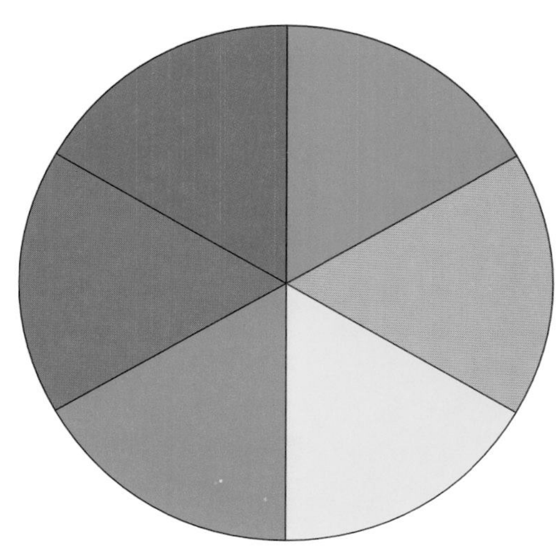

Create

How could you give a picture harmony with color? Create a harmonious picture.

1. Think about similar colors.
2. Color heavily on tagboard with similar bright crayons.
3. Cover the crayon with black paint. Let the paint dry, then use a paper clip to scratch out a picture.

Thomas Benton. Age 8. *The 4th of July.* Crayon and tempera.

Balancing Harmony and Variety

Monika Steinhoff. (American). *La Plazuela, La Fonda.* 1984. Oil on canvas. 24 × 20 inches. Courtesy of The Jamison Galleries, Santa Fe, New Mexico.

This artist paints things that are alike but different. How are they alike? How are they different? Do you think the likenesses and differences make the artwork interesting?

Seeing like an artist

Find objects in the room that are alike but different. Show them to the class.

Artists use **harmony** to unify an artwork. Harmony gives us the feeling that things go together.

Create

How can you balance harmony and variety in a mural? Draw or carve a tile for a class mural.

1. Think about a tile design.
2. Roll clay until it is $\frac{1}{4}$ inch thick. Cut out a geometric shape.
3. Draw or carve your design. Add clay and objects, or cut away clay, to add textures.

Rusty Cordone. Age 8. *Sunset.* Clay.

Unit 6 Lesson 6

Unity in Architecture

Frank Lloyd Wright/Gwathmey, Siegel, and Associates. (American). *The Solomon R. Guggenheim Museum.* Photograph by David Heald © The Solomon R. Guggenheim Foundation, New York, New York.

The original part of this museum is round. The new addition is a tall **rectangle**. The **architect** has united the old and new forms. What similarities do you see in the forms?

Seeing like an artist

Design a building with pattern blocks. Is the building harmonious? Does it have variety?

In art, **harmony** and **variety** must be balanced to create **unity**. Unity gives us the feeling that things belong together.

Create

What kind of sculpture can you create with recycled material? Design a sculpture with unity.

1. Think about what to make.
2. Choose sturdy objects to support your sculpture.
3. Glue forms together to make your sculpture. Then, paint the sculpture one color to create unity.

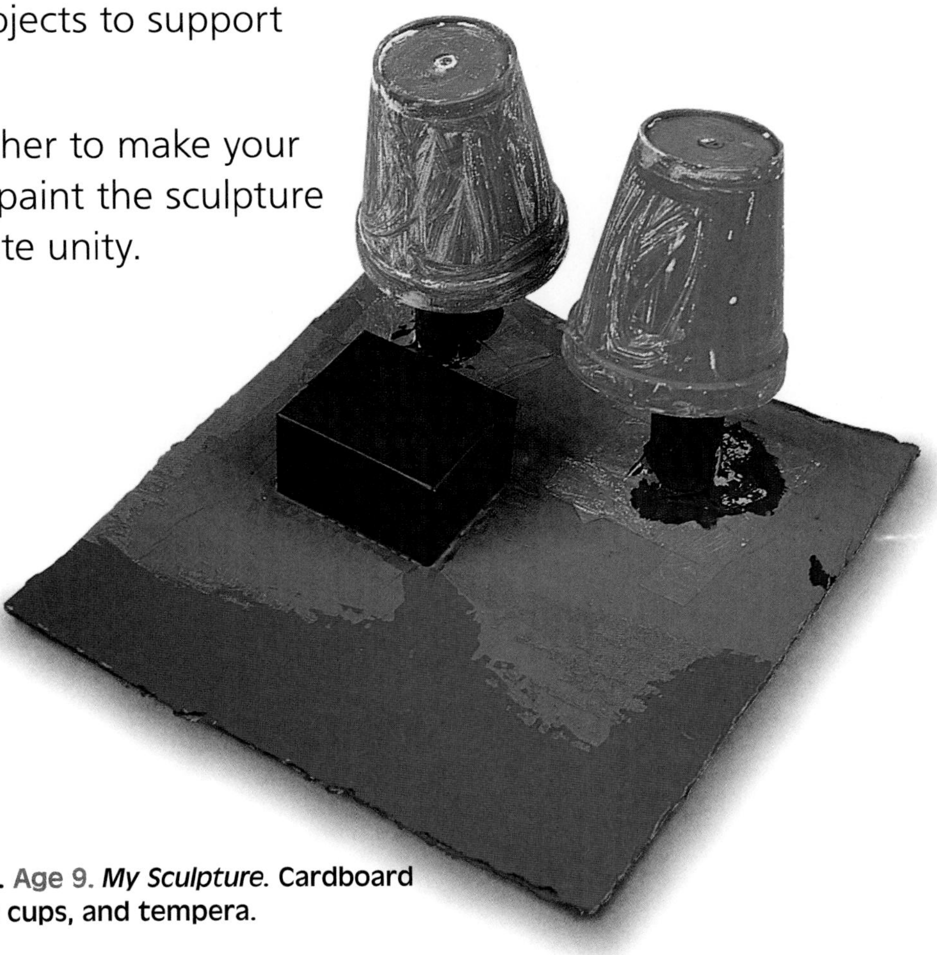

Matthew Cohan. Age 9. *My Sculpture.* Cardboard tubes, Styrofoam cups, and tempera.

Harmony, Variety, and Unity in Dance

Dance score of drawings for the dance "The Woolloomooloo Cuddle," An Air Mail Dance by Remy Charlip, ©1991.

Remy Charlip invented a dance. He gives people up to 40 drawings of dance positions. Each dancer can use the positions in any order. Dancers also choose their own music.

What To Do

Use your body to spell your name.

1. Print your first name. The letters have something in common. They are made with straight or curved lines.
2. Use your body to show the letters.
3. Find an interesting way to move from letter to letter.

Extra Credit

Teach your "Name Dance" to a partner. Learn his or her dance. Then spell out both names together.

Wrapping Up Unit 6

Harmony, Variety, and Unity

Reviewing Main Ideas

In art, harmony and variety must be balanced to create unity.

- Variety is differences.
- Harmony is a pleasing relationship created by repeating similar parts.
- Unity gives us a feeling that the parts of a work of art belong together.

Jean Dubuffet. (French). *The Loud One* (Le Vociférant). 1973. Painted sheet metal. 88 × 58$\frac{1}{2}$ × 34 inches. Albright-Knox Art Gallery, Buffalo, New York, room of Contemporary Art Fund, 1941/©1998 Artists Rights Society (ARS), New York/ADGP, Paris.

Careers in Art

Albert Romero is a special effects artist. He works at Warner Brothers Studio in California. Romero uses computers and other equipment to make fantastic creatures.

Summing Up

***L**ook* at the artwork. The artist has balanced variety and harmony.

- What did he use to create variety?
- How did he create harmony?

Artists balance variety and harmony to give the artwork unity.

Albert Romero, special effects artist

More About...

Technique Tips

Drawing

Pencil

Blend with the side of the lead.

Shading

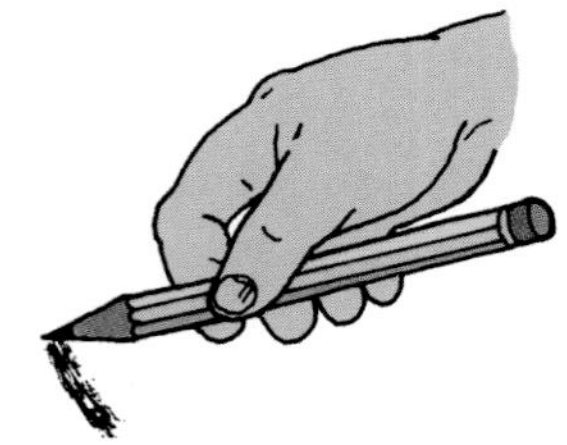

Hatching

Cross hatching

Stipple

Crayon

Make lines.

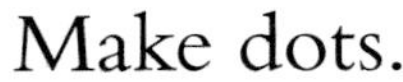

Make dots.

Color in large spaces.

Marker

Use the tip.

Use the tip side.

Always replace the cap.

More About...

Technique Tips

Oil Pastels

Make lines.

Color in large spaces.

Blend colors.

Colored Chalk

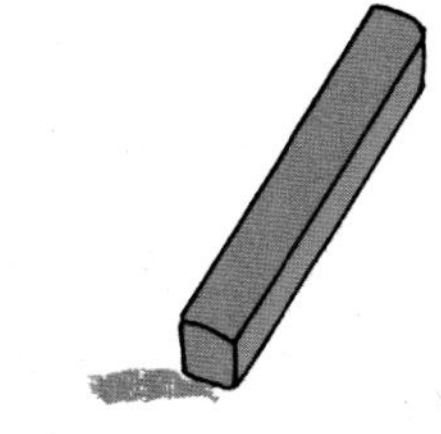
Make lines.

Color in large spaces.

Blend colors.

Painting

Taking Care of Your Paintbrush

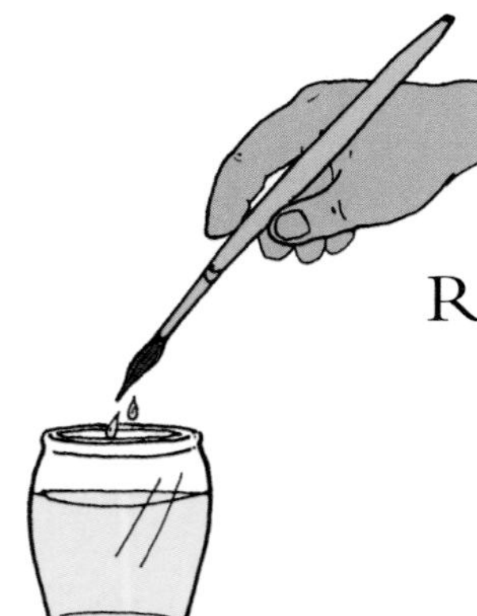

Rinse before using another color.
Blot on a paper towel.

Clean the brush after you paint.

1. Rinse.

2. Wash it with soap.

3. Rinse it again and blot.

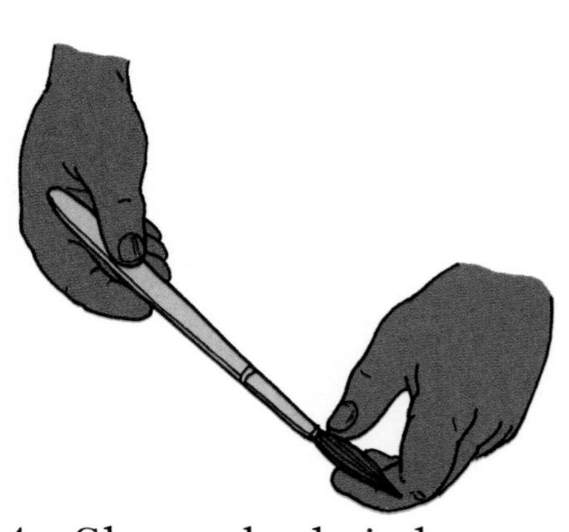

4. Shape the bristles.

5. Store with bristles up.

More About...
Technique Tips

Tempera

No drips or splatters.

Mix paint on a palette.

Wide brush for large areas.

Thin brush for details.

- For a fuzzy look, paint on dry paper with a damp brush.

Watercolors

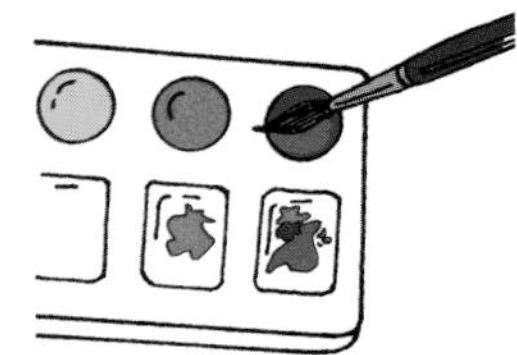

Put water on each color. Dip the brush in the paint.
Mix colors on a separate palette.

Thick lines.

Thin lines.

More About...
Technique Tips

Painting Texture with Watercolors

1. Dip in water.

2. Hold brush over container. Squeeze water out.

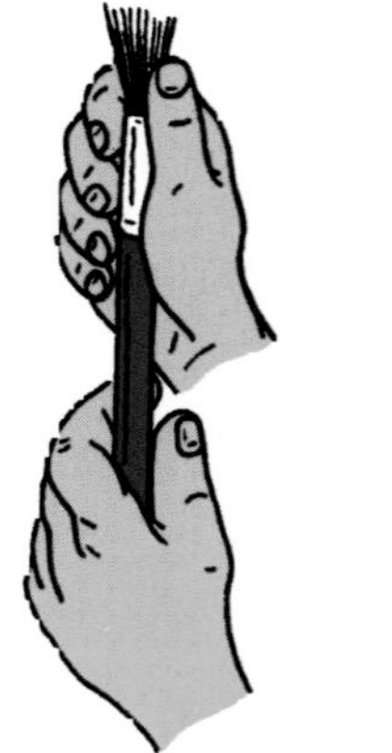

3. Divide into "spikes."

4. Dip in paint. Lightly touch to paper.

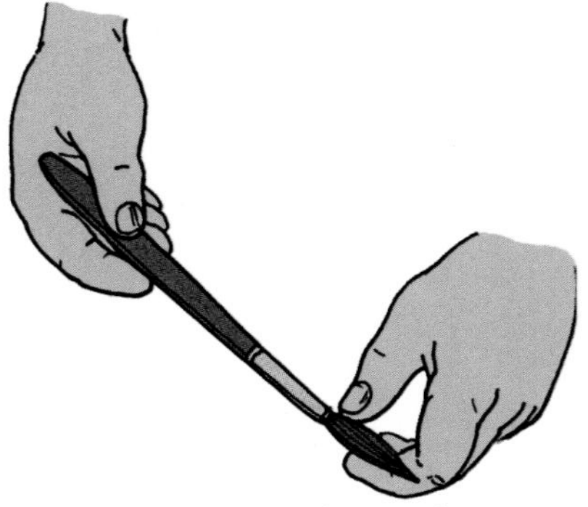

5. Rinse. Shape the bristles in a point.

Technique Tips

More About Watercolors

Add water to create a lighter value.
Add a bit of black to create a darker value.

- Paint on damp paper to create soft lines and soft edges. To make paper damp, tape it to a table. Brush clean water over the paper and let it soak in.

- Paint on dry paper to create sharp, clear lines and shapes.

Watercolor Resist

Crayons and oil pastels show through watercolor.

More About...

Technique Tips

Collage

Using Scissors

Always cut away from your body.

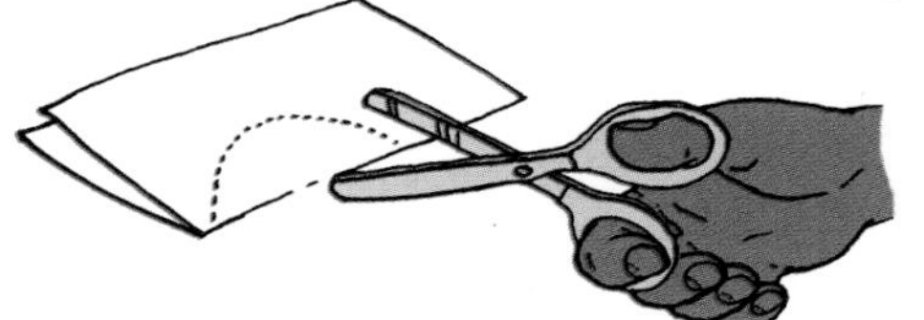

How to cut a shape from folded paper.

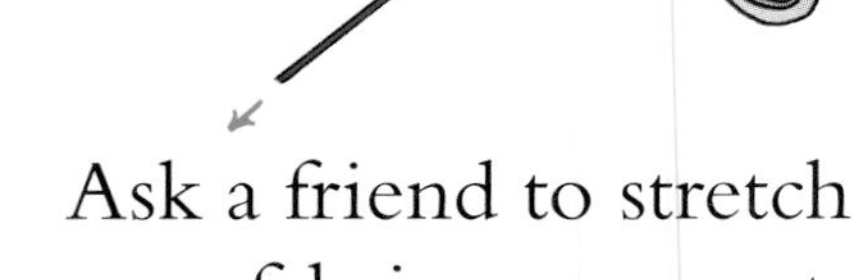

Ask a friend to stretch yarn or fabric as you cut.

Arranging a Design

Arrange pieces in a design. Glue them in place.

Using Glue

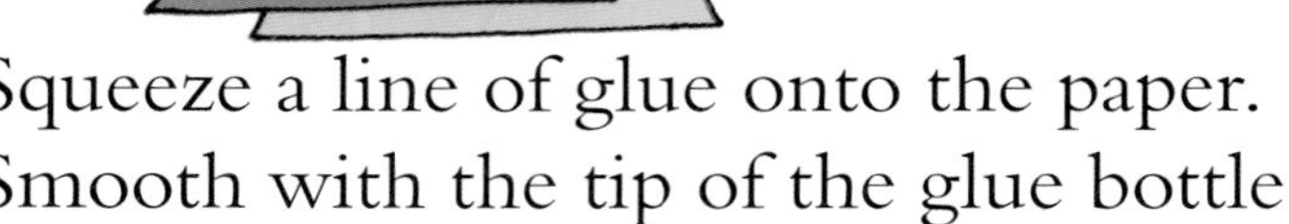

Squeeze a line of glue onto the paper. Smooth with the tip of the glue bottle.

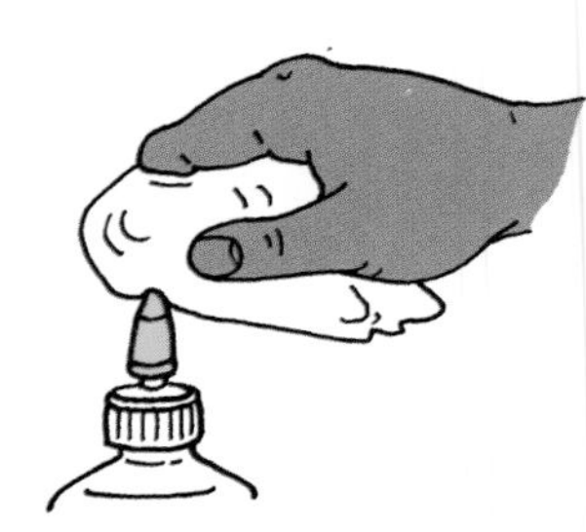

Clean the top and close the bottle when you are finished.

Technique Tips

Printmaking

Making a Sponge Print

Use a sponge for each color.
Dip a sponge in paint.
Press it onto paper.

Making a Stencil

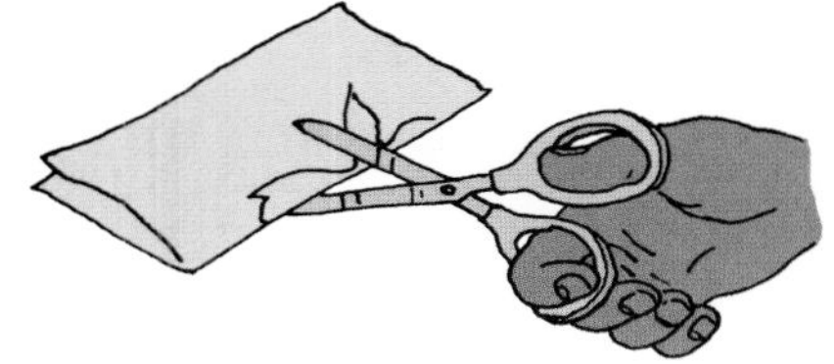

Cut a shape from folded paper.

The empty space is your stencil.

Sponge Printing with Stencils

Hold the stencil firmly in place.
Dip a sponge into paint.
Press it into the stencil.

Styrofoam Plate Printing

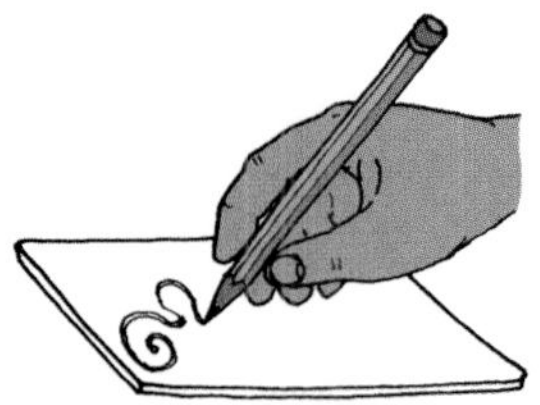

Etching

Inking the Brayer

Inking the Plate

Printing

Sculpting

Working with Clay

1. Form clay into an oval shape.

2. Squeeze a neck.

3. Pull out arms and legs.

4. Pull out legs and a tail for animals.

Joining Clay

To put two pieces of clay together:

1. *Score* or scratch both pieces so they stick together.

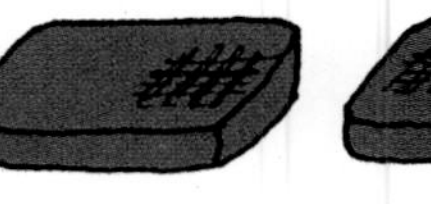

2. Put *slip* (liquid clay) on one piece with a brush.

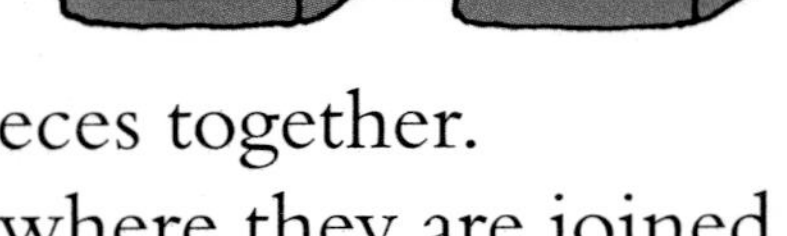

3. *Squeeze* the two pieces together. *Smooth* the pieces where they are joined.

Relief Tile

Paper Sculpture

Making Strip Forms

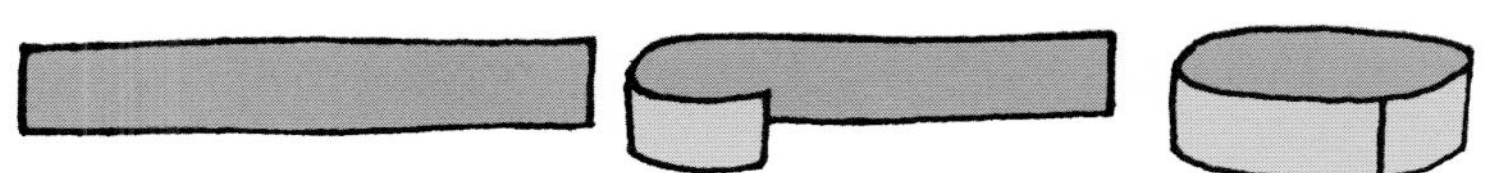

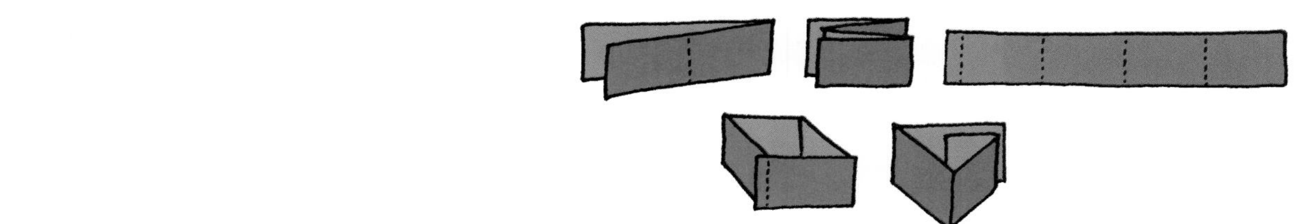

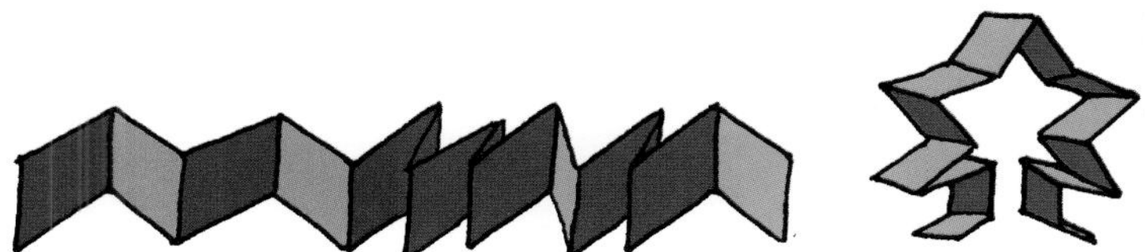

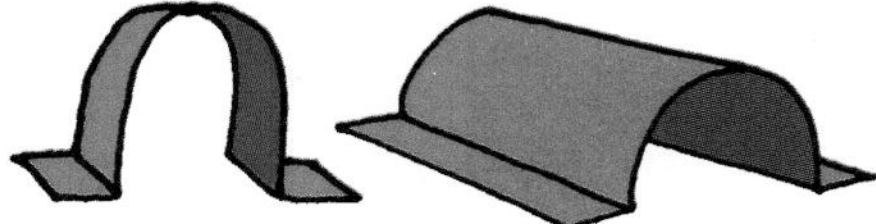

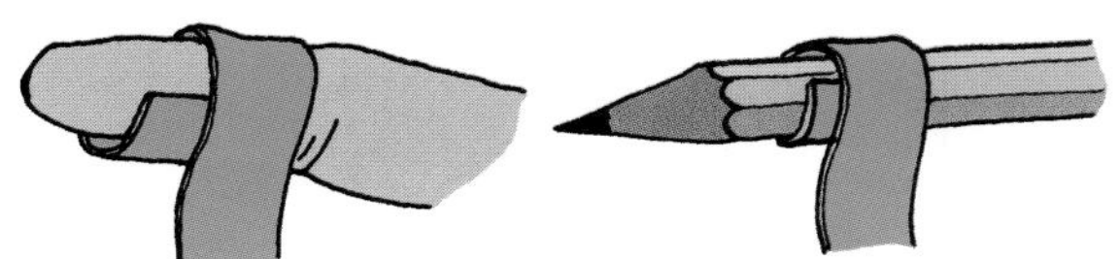

Use to make stairs, stars, fences, and other things.

Technique Tips

More Paper Sculpture

Making Cones

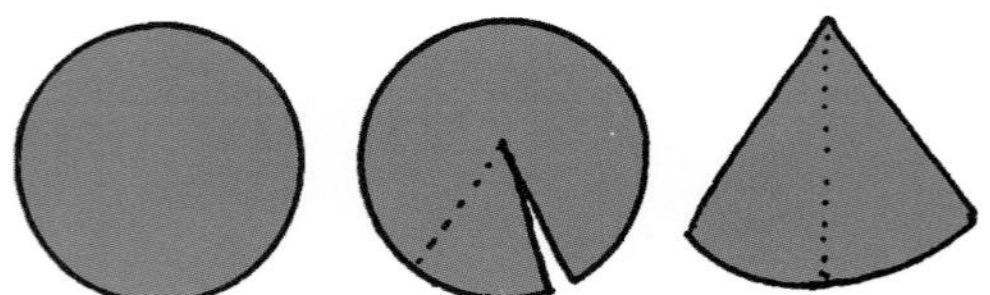

Making Masks

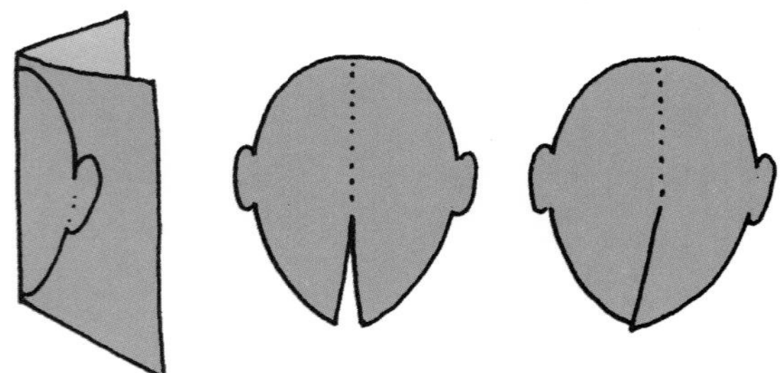

Building with Forms

More About...
Technique Tips

Needlework

The Running Stitch

Running Stitch

Weaving

Weaving a Belt

1. Pull yarn through straws.

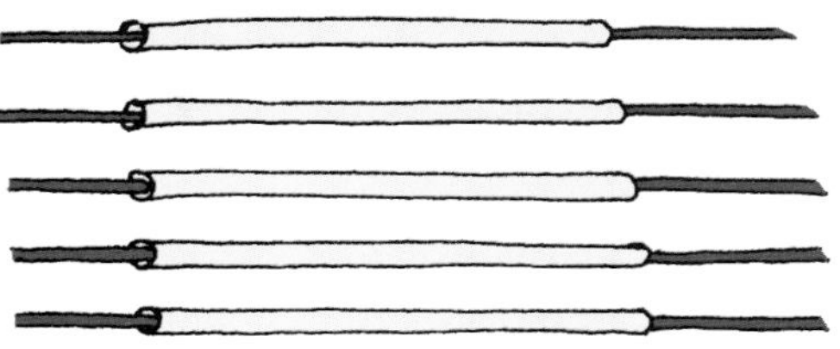

2. Knot ends.

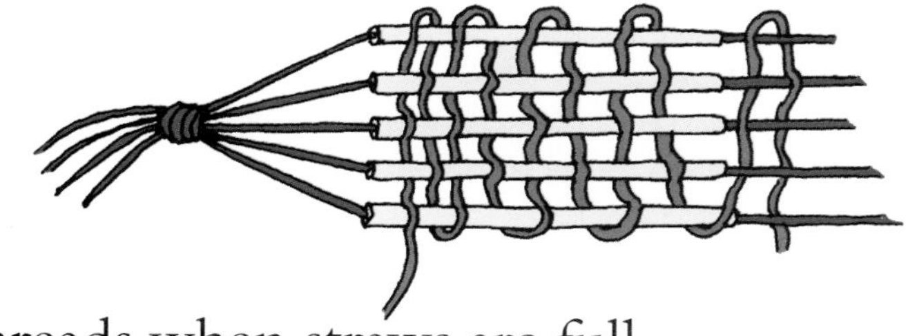

3. Weave over and under.

4. Push weft onto warp threads when straws are full.

More About...
Art Criticism

Francisco Goya. (Spanish). *Don Manuel Osorio Manrique de Zuñiga.* 1784. Oil on canvas. 50 × 40 inches. Metropolitan Museum of Art, New York, New York.

More About...
Art Criticism

DESCRIBE

List the people, animals, and things you see.

ANALYZE

What lines and shapes do you see?

What forms and spaces do you see?

What colors and values do you see?

How has the artist used rhythm, balance, and emphasis to organize this painting?

More About...
Art Criticism

Francisco Goya. (Spanish). *Don Manuel Osorio Manrique de Zuñiga.* 1784. Oil on canvas. 50 × 40 inches. Metropolitan Museum of Art, New York, New York.

More About...
Art Criticism

INTERPRET

What is happening? What is the artist telling you about this boy?

DECIDE

Have you ever seen another work of art like this?

LOOK

Look at the work of art.

Francisco Goya. (Spanish). *Don Manuel Osorio Manrique de Zuñiga.* 1784.
Oil on canvas. 50 × 40 inches. Metropolitan Museum of Art, New York, New York.

Aesthetics

LOOK AGAIN

Look at the work of art.

What sounds are in this work of art?

What smells are in this work of art?

What happened just before and just after in this work of art?

LOOK INSIDE

Look at the work of art.

Pretend you are Don Manuel. How do you feel?

Do you like wearing those clothes?

Tell a story about this work with a beginning, a middle, and an end.

Francisco Goya. (Spanish). *Don Manuel Osorio Manrique de Zuñiga.* 1784. Oil on canvas. 50 × 40 inches. Metropolitan Museum of Art, New York, New York.

More About...
Aesthetics

LOOK OUTSIDE

Look at the work of art.

How is this like or different from your own life?

How would you change this work of art to be more like your life? What would the changes be? What would the artwork look like?

What will you remember about this work?

More About...
Art History

Artist unknown.
Pagoda of the Temple of the Six Banyon Trees.
A.D. 537. China.

Artist unknown.
Notre Dame de Paris. (South Flank).
1400s. France.

Artist unknown.
Tutankhamen Mask (side view) Cover.
1340 B.C. Egypt.

Artist unknown.
Parthenon. 448–432 B.C. Greece.

15,000 B.C.–A.D. 1400

Artist unknown.
Stonehenge.
1800–1400 B.C. England.

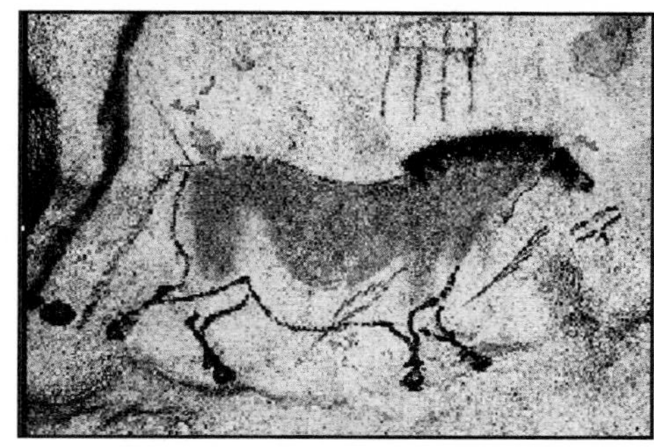

Artist unknown.
Yellow Horse. (Chinese Horse). 15,000–10,000 B.C. France.

Artist unknown.
Adena Effigy figure.
1000–300 B.C.
United States.

Artist unknown.
Haniwa Horse.
A.D. 400–500. Japan.

Artist unknown.
Ravenna Apse Mosaic.
(Detail.) A.D. 100. Italy.

Artist unknown.
Shiva, Lord of the Dance.
A.D. 1000. India.

More About...
Art History

Leonardo da Vinci.
Mona Lisa. 1503.
Italy.

Claude Monet.
Impression, Sunrise.
1872. France.

Michelangelo.
Head of David.
Italy.

Albrecht Dürer.
Self-Portrait.
1500s. Germany.

Jan Vermeer.
Girl with the Red Hat. 1660s.
Holland.

late 1400s–Present

Artist unknown.
Taj Mahal.
1632–1648. India.

Vincent van Gogh.
Bedroom at Arles.
1888. Holland.

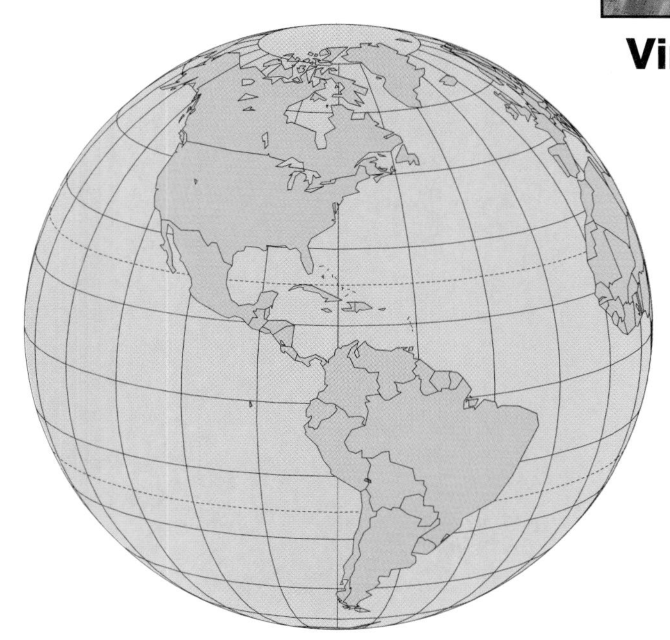

Pablo Picasso.
Gertrude Stein.
1906. Spain.

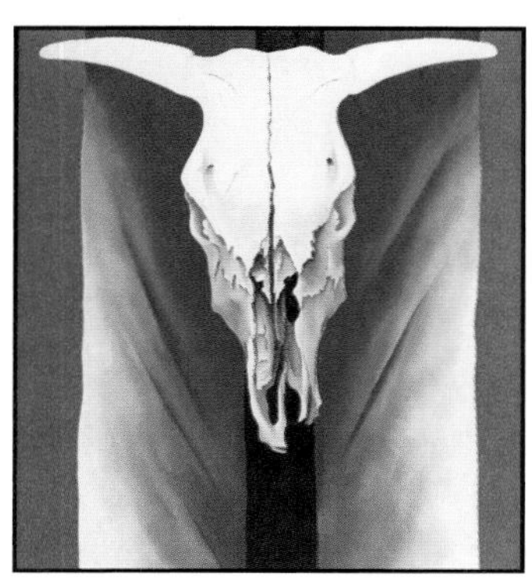

Georgia O'Keeffe.
Cow's Skull, Red, White, and Blue.
1931. United States.

Marc Chagall.
Peasant Life.
Russia.

More About...
Subject Matter

Artists create art about many subjects. Point to the different subject matter you see.

Landscape

Henri Rousseau. (French). *Carnival Evening.* 1886. Oil on canvas. $46 \times 35\frac{1}{4}$ inches. Philadelphia Museum of Art, The Louis E. Stern Collection, Philadelphia, Pennsylvania.

More About...
Subject Matter

Portrait

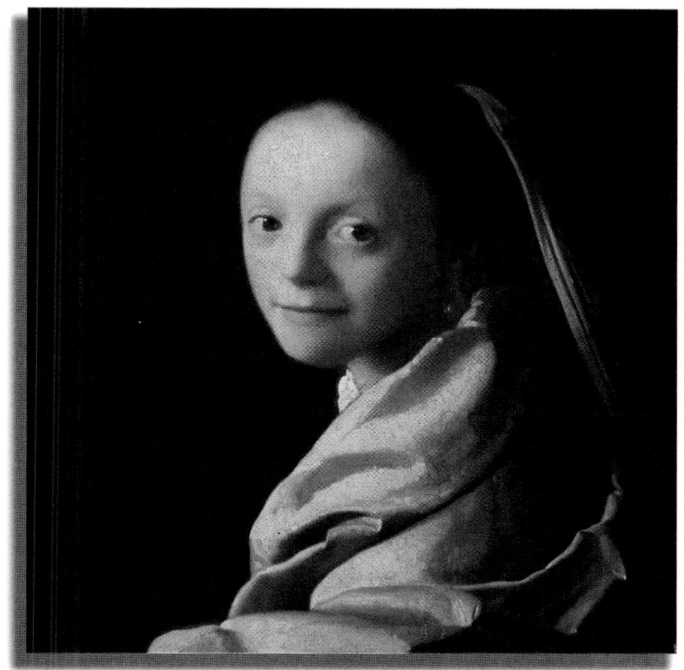

Jan Vermeer. (Dutch). *Portrait of a Young Woman.* Oil on canvas.

Still Life

Ignace Henri Fantin-Latour. (French). *Still Life with Flowers and Fruit.* 1866. Oil on canvas. $28\frac{3}{4} \times 23\frac{5}{8}$ inches. Metropolitan Museum of Art, NY.

More About...

Subject Matter

Art with a Deeper Meaning

Nicodemus Lopez. (American). *Saint George and the Dragon.* Philadelphia Museum of Art. Philadelphia, Pennsylvania.

A Story

Marc Chagall. (Russian). *Birthday.* 1915. Oil on cardboard. $31\frac{3}{4} \times 39\frac{1}{4}$ inches. The Museum of Modern Art, New York. ©1998 Artists Rights Society (ARS), New York/ADAGP, Paris.

More About...
Subject Matter

Colors, Lines, and Shapes

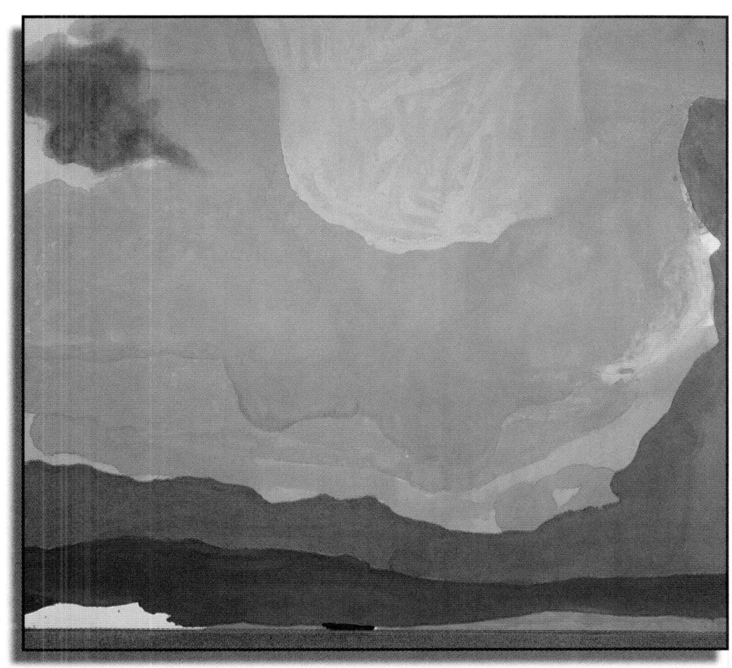

Helen Frankenthaler. (American). *Flood.* 1967. Synthetic polymer on canvas. The Whitney Museum of Art, New York, New York.

Everyday Activities

John Singer Sargent. (American). *Carnation, Lily, Lily, Rose.* The Tate Gallery, London, England. Art Resource, NY.

More About...

Seeing Form

Most pictures you see have forms you already know.

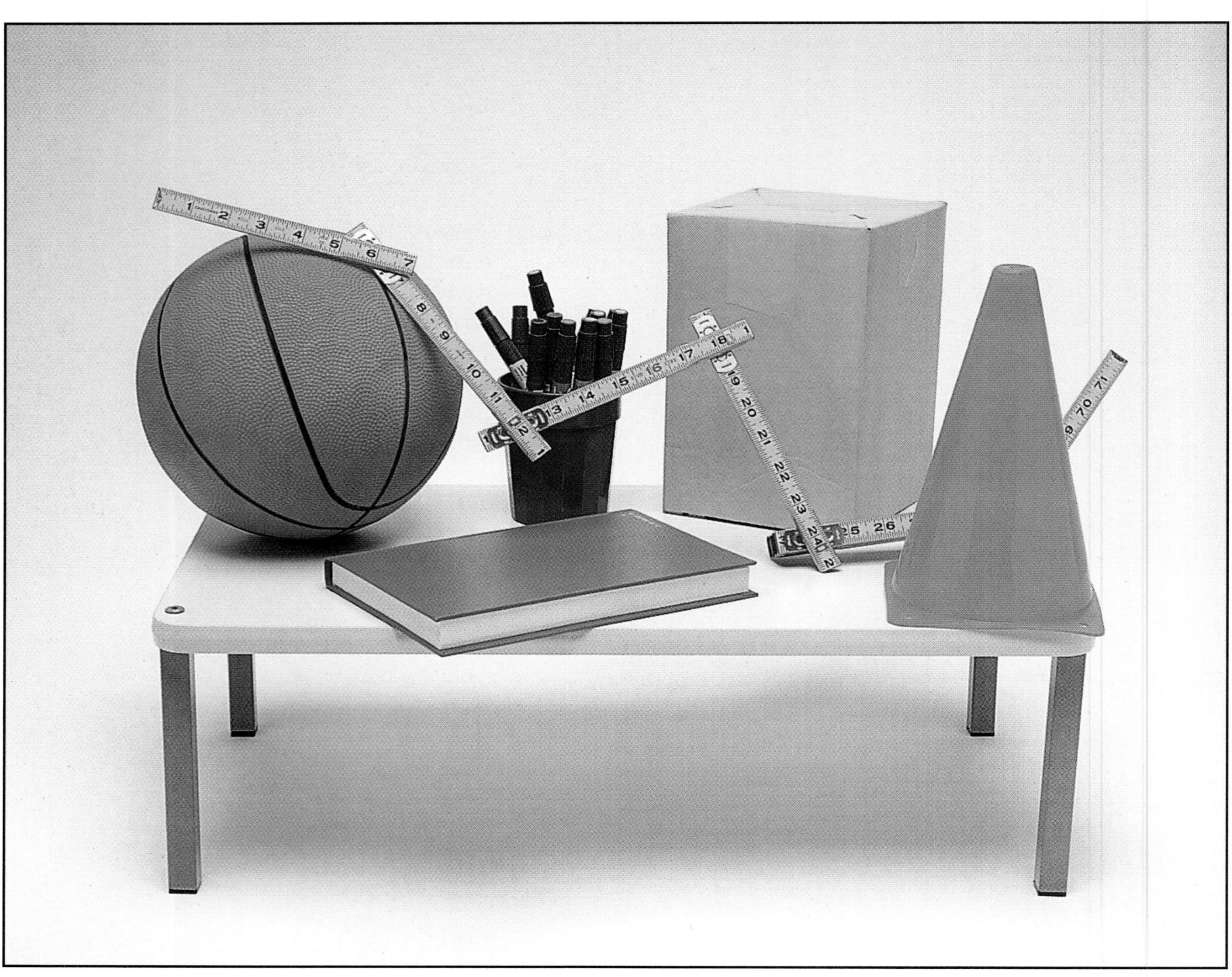

More About...

Seeing Form

LOOK

Where are these forms in the picture?

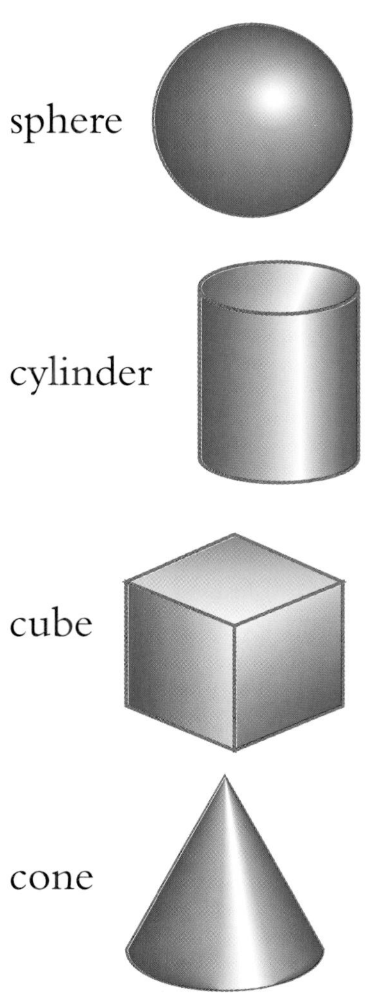

What shape is like a sphere?
What shape is most like the side of a cylinder?

Name the shape on the front of the cube.
What shape is similar to a cone?

More About...
Seeing Space

Most pictures have empty and filled spaces.

More About...
Seeing Space

LOOK

Find an empty space in the picture.

Where is the empty triangle?

Where is an empty rectangle?

Describe the shape of the space under the bus.

Do the children have any space between them?

Find more examples of space in your classroom.

More About...
Seeing Texture

How would things feel in this picture if you could touch them?

More About...
Seeing Texture

LOOK

Describe the texture of the ground.

How does the horse's mane look like it would feel?

How would the surface of the horse's nose feel?

What is the texture of the water?

How is the texture different from the ground?

Describe textures in your classroom.

Visual Index: Artworks Arranged in Time Order

Artist unknown
Gui Ritual Food Container
Eleventh century B.C.
page 86

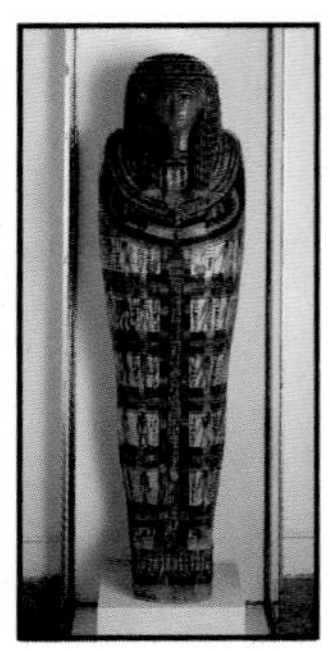

Artist unknown
Egyptian Mummy Case
c. 945–715 B.C.
page 88

Artist unknown
Pantheon
A.D. 118–128
page 32

Thomas Affleck
Side Chair
1770
page 90

Artist unknown
Delaware Shoulder Bag
c. 1860
page 72

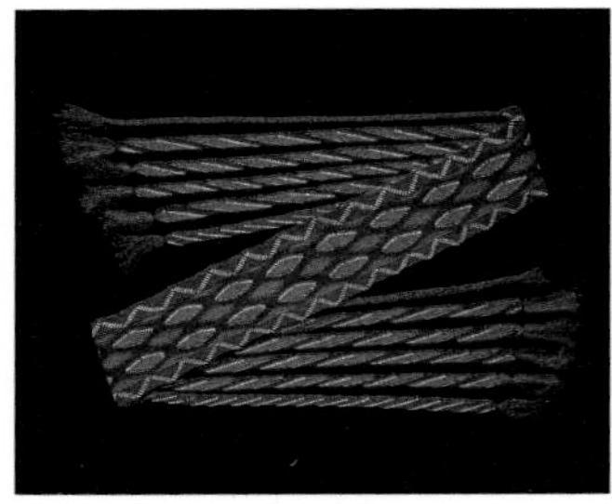

Artist unknown
Sash
1885
page 94

Visual Index

Vincent van Gogh
The Starry Night
1889
page 70

Claude Monet
Poplars on the Epte
1891
page 18

James J. Shannon
Jungle Tales
1895
page 38

Harriet Powers
Pictorial Quilt (detail: Falling Stars 1894–95)
1895–1898
page 92

Paul Cézanne
Still Life with Apples
1895–1898
page 40

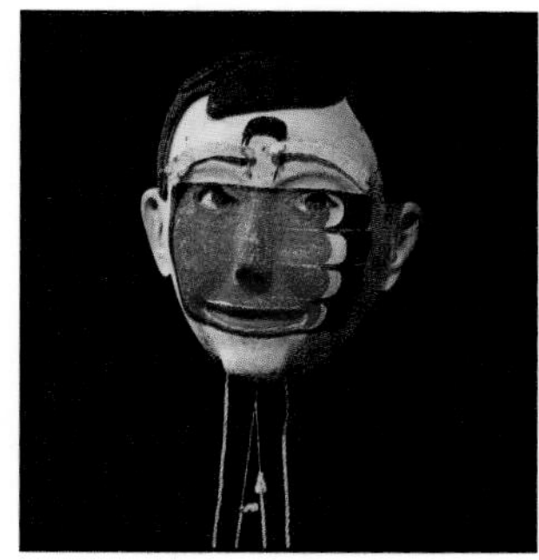

Artist Unknown
Self-Portrait Mask
Pre-twentieth century
page 34

Visual Index

Virginia Caswell
Bullwinkle of the Sea
Twentieth century
page 96

Edward Steichen
The Flatiron–Evening
1904
page 52

Wassily Kandinsky
Composition IV
1913
page 20

Tom Thomson
Spring Ice
1916
page 60

Paul Klee
The Tree of Houses
1918
page 104

Joseph Stella
The Voice of the City of New York/The White Way 1
1920–1922
page 16

Visual Index

Thomas Hart Benton
I Got a Girl on Sourwood Mountain
1938
page 68

Adolph Gottlieb
Spectre of the Sea
1947
page 56

Auguste Herbin
Composition on the Word "Vie" 2
1950
page 22

Artist unknown
Indonesian Shadow Puppet
c. 1950
page 24

Louise Nevelson
Dawn's Wedding Chapel II
1959
page 78

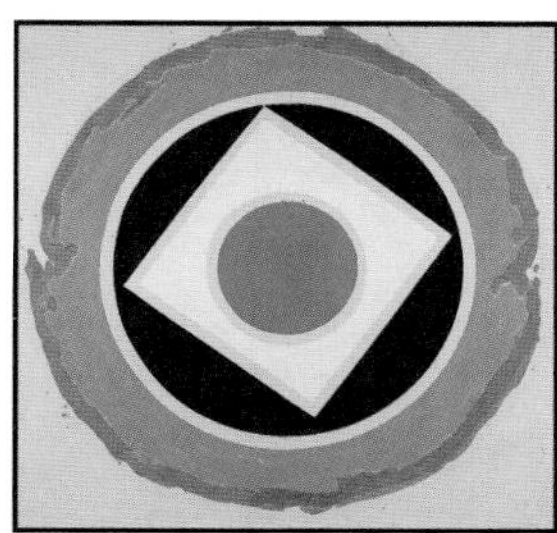

Kenneth Noland
Split
1959
page 108

Visual Index

Artist unknown
Votive Horse
1960
page 42

Heron Martínez
Church
c. 1960
page 14

Romare Bearden
Return of the Prodigal Son
1967
page 106

Patrick Des Jarlait
Gathering Wild Rice
1972
page 58

Ivan Eyre
Touchwood Hills
1972–1973
page 110

Suad al-Attar
Untitled/Iraq
1981
page 76

Visual Index

Monika Steinhoff
La Plazuela, La Fonda
1984
page 112

Robert Lostutter
Baird Trogon
1985
page 50

Roxanne Swentzell
The Emergence of the Clowns
1988
page 36

Jane Wilson
Solstice
1991
page 54

Frank Lloyd Wright/
Gwathmey, Siegel, & Associates
The Solomon R. Guggenheim Museum
1992
page 114

Peggy Flora Zalucha
Peony Blooms (IX)
1992
page 74

Glossary

active lines

Lines that show action and add energy to a work of art. Diagonal, zigzag and curved lines are active lines.

architect

An artist that designs and plans the construction of buildings.

broken line

circle

collage

Bits and pieces of things glued onto paper.

color wheel

A way of organizing spectral colors in a circle.

contrast

Difference between things next to each other in an artwork.

cool hues

Blue, green, and violet. Another name for *cool colors*.

cool colors

Blue, green, and violet.

curved (curving) line

depth

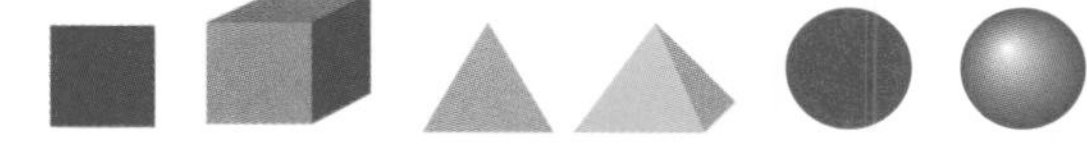

Glossary

diagonal (line)

dimension

Height or width or depth.

emphasis

Stress as important.

fabric

Cloth.

formal balance

When both halves are the same.

free-form

An irregular shape.

free-form shape

A shape that is not geometric. It is irregular.

geometric shape

harmonious

When things seem to go together.

harmony

A pleasing relationship between parts of an artwork.

height

How tall something is.

horizontal (line)

Glossary

hue

Another word for color.

line

mask

Art made to be worn over the face.

mood

How an artwork makes you feel.

motif

mural

A painting done on a wall.

overlap

When one thing is put over another.

photographer

Artist that takes pictures with a camera.

primary hues

Red, blue and yellow.

rectangle

rhythm

Patterns.

rough line

Glossary

sarcophagus

A mummy case.

sculpture

A three-dimensional work of art.

secondary hue

A mixture of two primary hues. Orange, green, and violet are secondary hues.

shade

Dark values of a color.

shape

A flat, two-dimensional figure.

smooth line

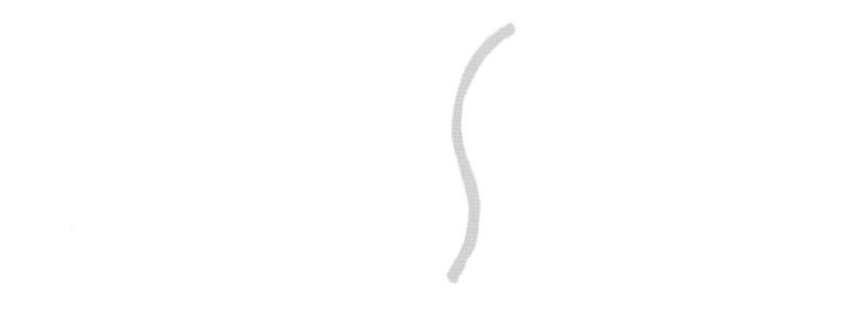

solid line

square

still life

Collection of objects that do not move.

swirling line

symmetry

When halves of a design are mirror images of each other.

tactile texture

Texture you can feel.

Glossary

texture

Something you can feel or looks like you can feel.

thick line

thin line

three-dimensional

Having height, width and depth.

tint

Light values of a color.

triangle

two-dimensional

Having height and width.

unity

The feeling that parts of an artwork belong together.

value

Lightness or darkness of a color.

variety

The use of different lines, shapes, and colors in artwork.

vertical (line)

Glossary

visual movement

The movement of your eyes through a work of art.

visual pattern

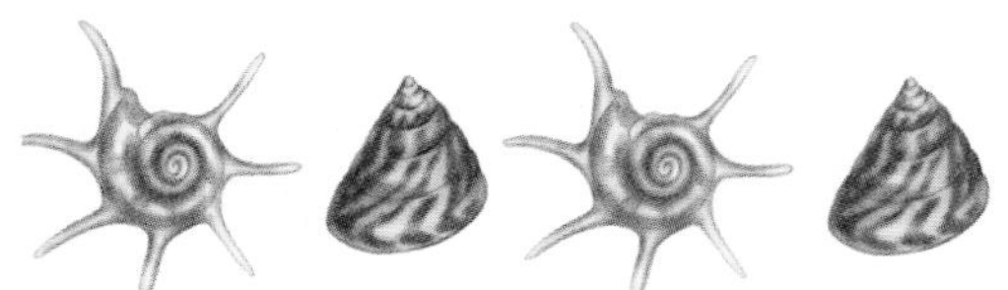

visual rhythm

visual texture

Texture you can see, but cannot feel.

warm hues

Yellow, orange, and red.

width

How wide something is.

zigzag (line)

Index

Index

Index